SO-BNS-879

Shirley Carter
8/11

So You Want to Teach, Eh?

Shirley A. Artson

iUniverse, Inc.
New York   Bloomington

Copyright © 2010 by Shirley A. Artson

All rights reserved. No part of this book may be used or reproduced by any means, graphic, electronic, or mechanical, including photocopying, recording, taping or by any information storage retrieval system without the written permission of the publisher except in the case of brief quotations embodied in critical articles and reviews.

iUniverse books may be ordered through booksellers or by contacting:

iUniverse
1663 Liberty Drive
Bloomington, IN 47403
www.iuniverse.com
1-800-Authors (1-800-288-4677)

Because of the dynamic nature of the Internet, any Web addresses or links contained in this book may have changed since publication and may no longer be valid. The views expressed in this work are solely those of the author and do not necessarily reflect the views of the publisher, and the publisher hereby disclaims any responsibility for them.

ISBN: 978-1-4401-9592-1 (sc)
ISBN: 978-1-4401-9594-5 (hc)
ISBN: 978-1-4401-9593-8 (ebook)

Printed in the United States of America

iUniverse rev. date: 03/08/2010

Introduction

I discovered very early in my career that teaching was my niche. However, during my first year I nearly lost my enthusiasm because of the lack of support and resources and the unrealistic demands.

It quickly became apparent to me that in order to be effective in the classroom, a person must be emotionally and physically strong, willing to make personal sacrifices, and able to work around the numerous barriers that teachers encounter.

I am sharing my teaching experiences hoping to pave the way for those seriously considering the teaching profession and to encourage those currently working in the profession.

One

I stood before the class of forty eighth graders, many of whom were over the age of sixteen. They'd entered my classroom like gangbusters and now sat staring at me with hostile expressions: arms folded tightly across chests or arms propping up heads, with elbows resting on desks. Not one student smiled. Their postures reflected a lack of interest in anything that I'd planned to present. I soon realized that I was out of my element. I was as uncomfortable as a fish out of water. I tried to greet the class, but my throat was as dry as the Mohave Desert. I swallowed hard. "Good morning, class," I finally said.

At thirty-nine years old, I was the mother of five children, a senior in college, and separated from my husband, who'd left us for romance with a pretty young thing. My changed circumstances presented me with a dilemma: How was I going to support my children? I prayed and asked God to help me. Be careful what you pray for; you just might get it!

One day I received a call from the English coordinator for the Baltimore City Public Schools. She told me that the school system was hiring college graduates who did not have a teaching certificate but were interested in teaching. I could be hired as a provisional teacher, she said, and work while obtaining my teaching certification. I needed a job. So I thought about it and decided to accept the position.

I didn't realize at the time that I was accepting the calling of my life. I believed I was accepting the position out of the need to provide for my children. Also, teaching would allow me to work the same hours as my children's school hours, and when school was closed for snow days or holidays, I would be also off work and not need a sitter. The job was the answer to my prayers. I don't recall if I was excited about it at the time, but I remember that it solved my immediate problem; that was a great relief. However, later I came to realize that teaching was my calling.

When I allowed myself to think about it later—before I met my first class—I thought it was going to be an easy job. The supervisors who hired me knew that I had no teaching experience or training. I thought it would be a piece of cake. I would stand before the class, present the lesson, and the students would raise their hands, anxious to participate. So you can imagine my shock when I realized that was not at all the case.

I began my teaching career during the late 1970s. I was assigned to the School of Hard Knocks in southeast Baltimore, a junior high school in an enormous building with three levels that accommodated more than twelve hundred students, grades seven through nine. It had the reputation of being one of the toughest junior high schools in the city. The students were known for being streetwise, unruly, undisciplined, and very uncooperative. Of course, no one shared those facts when I accepted the position. There were three assistant principals; one assigned to each grade level. Mrs. Mildred Glad was the seventh-grade assistant principal; Mr. Moodi Paine, the eighth-grade assistant principal; and Mr. George Amigo, the ninth-grade assistant principal. Each was responsible for the students assigned to his or her respective grade level.

The new school year had been in session for one week. During the second week of school, I was given an appointment to meet with the principal, Mr. Nomis Eergel. I arrived on time for my 1 PM appointment. As I made my way to the main office, I passed a man in the hall who was strongly disciplining a male student. I didn't know at the time that he was the principal. Short in stature, with a no-nonsense demeanor, he was telling the young man what he would and would not do if he was going to remain at the School of Hard Knocks.

I entered the main office and stood at the long counter for several minutes before one of the secretaries acknowledged my presence. I stated my name, and I was told by one of the secretaries that the principal was in the hall, so I should have a seat and wait for his return. Within five minutes, the principal came into the office. I immediately recognized him as the person I'd seen in the hall. The secretary informed him that I was the new English teacher and that I was there for an appointment with him.

He looked me up and down. His facial expression revealed that he had reservations about me filling the position, but he extended his hand, smiled, and invited me to follow him to his office. I glanced back at the office staff. Their expressions mirrored the principal's, a sort of *oh my God* look. I wasn't sure exactly what the expression meant, so I chose to ignore it. Later I realized that the expressions meant that they were questioning how long I would last.

In the office, Mr. Eergel invited me to have a seat and said, "So you want to teach, eh?" The emphasis was on *you*. We had a very brief meeting. When it the ended he handed me a binder. "This is a copy of the school handbook. Read it when you get a chance. You'll want to become familiar with the procedures and rules. Here are the keys to your classroom and the teachers' lavatory. Go up the steps outside of the main office, turn right, and go to the end of the hall. Room 140 is your classroom. After you've seen your room, if you'll come back to office, I'll introduce you to the English department head," he said.

I entered my classroom and found the room in disarray. Student desks and chairs were all over the place, and several balls of paper were on the floor. The teacher's desk was in a corner with textbooks stacked on top. The bulletin boards were bare, the chalkboard covered with graffiti. I don't know what I was expecting to see, but I was disappointed. I stood there looking around the room for a moment. It didn't look like much, but it felt good to stand in the middle of my first classroom and daydream a bit. I placed the handbook on the teacher's desk, left the room, and returned to the principal's office.

Mrs. Helen Scottie was introduced to me as the English department head. She wore an attitude of mild annoyance. After the introduction, she escorted me to her office on the third level. She didn't say very much. In fact, she seemed displeased about the interruption to her day. She gave me a three-inch binder. Her tone of voice reflected her irritation. "This is the eighth-grade curriculum that we must follow. Make sure that you write an objective on the board every day. Make sure you have class work and a drill every day and that you assign homework daily."

She continued telling me to make sure to do this, that, and the other. She gave me a long list of "make sures," and she ended with, "I'll see you in the morning." I left her office and returned to my classroom. I sat at the desk and thought, *God must really have a good sense of humor; I am expected to teach without any training.*

That was my introduction to teaching and to the school. No one gave me the essential tools, such as class rosters, the bell schedule, or a tour of the building. I had to learn my way around the huge building on my own. The only things I received were a curriculum binder, an outdated handbook, a set of keys, and a long verbal list of "make sures." I was not told what to do when meeting my classes the next day. God had answered my prayer, so I decided not to be upset about the situation. I just prayed for guidance.

I was not certified to teach. I had just graduated from college the June before classes began that September. I knew absolutely nothing about teaching. I was very apprehensive, but I'd committed to taking the job.

After a few moments I reassured myself, *This can't be so bad. After all, I was hired without training, formal or otherwise.* I decided that it was going to be all right. I'd stand before the class, tell the students what I wanted them to do, and they'd do what I asked. I'd go over the work, grade it, and return it to the students. Everybody would be happy. Little did I know, I was in for the shock of my life.

I will never forget my first day on the job. I was excited that morning. I got up early, bathed, and dressed. I prepared breakfast for my children and saw my teens off to school. Then I slipped on my high heels, threw my purse strap over my shoulder, looked in the mirror a couple times, picked up my briefcase, and left the house. I felt exhilarated. I had prepared a lesson for the day the night before. I was as prepared as possible to meet my students. I dropped my younger children off at their elementary school and proceeded on to work in my 1961 Ford Falcon. I felt great! It was my first job after graduating from college. The world seemed a much brighter place. I sang along with the radio and smiled nearly all the way to work.

I arrived to school early, ready to meet my wonderful students. Mr. Eergel was at the front door greeting teachers. He met me with a smile. "Good morning, Mrs. Artson. We're glad to have you. Enjoy your first day." With a cheerful smile and tone, I replied, "Thank you." I walked the hall toward my classroom along with the other teachers, opened my classroom door, stood there looking around, and felt lost. Suddenly my confidence was gone, and I realized that I didn't know what to do. I'd had the crash course of "make sures"; I had the curriculum binder and the school handbook. Now what was I to do? I felt little quivers of panic in my belly. I thought, *Oh my God! What have I gotten myself into, and how do I get out of it?* It no longer felt like it was going to be all right. I talked to myself about my abilities, and I prayed, but fear was now my enemy. I was experiencing the "suppose this and suppose that" syndrome.

I sat at my desk for a few moments, paced around the room in circles, took several slow deep breaths, and forced myself to relax. I told myself to calm down. Once I had regained my composure, I recalled Mrs. Scottie's directives to write the activities for the day on the chalkboard. My lesson plan was based on the curriculum.

I was prepared with a drill, a class activity, and a homework assignment. I wrote the activities on the board.

I hoped that Mrs. Scottie would stop by before the students arrived to give me the class lists and the bell schedule. Suddenly, I started feeling anxious again. I was concerned about the lesson I'd prepared. I'd followed the directions given to me, but I felt uncertain. I heard Mrs. Scottie's voice in my mind's ear: "Make sure you have work on the board for the students." It was hard to remember all the "make sures," but I did my best.

I managed to maintain my courage and was ready to meet my first class. I had been told that I must stand at my classroom door to welcome the students as they arrived and to usher them into the room. They stared at me as they approached. After a while, I began to feel a bit uneasy because their expressions were not friendly. Their faces revealed misgivings, as if asking, "Who the heck are you, and what do think you're going to do?" These students had already been without a teacher for an entire week and had become accustomed to doing what pleased them; they obviously wanted to continue doing so. Finally, the halls were clear; all the students were in their respective classrooms.

I closed my door and, with a welcoming smile on my face, I was ready to greet my class. They looked me over, and I looked them over. In those days, African American students wore huge afro hair styles, long but curly, and they would pick their hair out into a large, rounded shape that surrounded their faces. The boys wore colorful sleeveless silk undershirts and stuffed the matching tee-shirts into their back pockets. They wore jeans that sat low on their hips, several pairs of socks pushed down and bulging around their ankles like an inflated tire, and athletic shoes. The girls also wore their hair in big afros. Their attire was skirts, blouses or polo shirts, and knee socks pushed down to their ankles. They also wore the popular athletic shoes of the day. The students' expressions and their body language were almost terrifying. They seemed to be saying, "Go ahead, teach me. I dare you." This was my first encounter with my eighth-grade students. I didn't have a clue as to what to do with them, and they sensed it. Somehow, I made it through the day without incident.

Mrs. Scottie did not stop by the entire day. I gave myself a pat on the back for surviving. I stood in the middle of the room and thought, *What the heck am I doing here, really?* I honestly could not answer the question then. However, here I am thirty years later, a retired teacher, now able to answer the question. I came to teaching out of need. I know now that I stayed for love of the art of teaching. It had to be either love or insanity, because my first year was so stressful that when I think back now I truly wonder how I made it through. However, I do not think it was much different for me that first year than for most teachers. As a new teacher, you don't know what to do or who to ask for help. You do not dare ask for help too often for fear that you'll be considered weak or incompetent. That's what administrators sometimes project. They may not do it intentionally, but the thought hangs out there. *You don't know what to do?* Your teaching performance and competence become questionable in their eyes. I was as reluctant to ask for help as most new teachers.

I soon found myself experiencing difficulty. I was struggling with the curriculum and the lessons. I was struggling with classroom management. I was struggling with the classroom environment. I was even struggling with simple things like making my room attractive and inviting.

Neither my department head, the English specialist, nor the administrator offered any assistance. They didn't stop by to check my progress. They left me floundering on my own. Like a non-swimmer in an ocean, I was sinking fast.

Help finally came in the persons of two seasoned teachers whose classrooms were across the hall from mine. One day they came to my room to welcome me to the school. They looked around the room but didn't say a word about the appearance of it. For background paper, I had fastened red crepe paper to the bulletin boards with tacks. I had not used border strips. I had not put anything else on the boards because I didn't know what I should put there. I'd walked through the halls and peeped in classrooms and noticed that other teachers had colored paper and borders on their bulletin boards. Their boards looked very nice, but mine looked terrible.

Finally, one of the teachers, Mrs. Charity, spoke. "I see you're trying to get your room together. Would you like some help?" I was so happy that I actually embraced her. She just smiled and told me to follow her. She escorted me to her room, pointed out what she had done to her boards, and explained how she did it. Then, Mrs. Kinder escorted me next door to her room and told me what she'd done with her boards. They told me that if I would purchase the things I needed to fix my boards, they would help me. They also told me exactly what I needed to purchase for my bulletin boards and where to purchase the materials. Happy as a rat with a gold tooth, I rejoiced as I left the room, extremely grateful.

I did not realize that there was actually a correct way to set up bulletin boards. That afternoon I went to the teachers' resource store and purchased all the supplies the teachers had listed for me. Who knew that there was such a place as a teachers' resource store? It was a wonderful place! There were books of all kinds and for every skill. There was bulletin board paper in many colors and shades, posters, border strips galore, and everything imaginable that teachers on all levels might need. I purchased the items on my list and left, knowing that I would soon return.

I arrived early the next morning, as did my two heroines, and we began the task of preparing my bulletin boards. They helped me choose the best background paper and border for each bulletin board. They also helped me decide which posters were best. We completed a subject bulletin board, a class rules and procedures board, an announcements board, and a board to showcase students' work. My room suddenly looked so nice. It was brighter and felt warm and welcoming. I hugged both teachers and gave them a heartfelt thank-you.

Bulletin boards were not my only problem. I did not know what an instructional objective was or how to write one. Mrs. Scottie came to my room during the second week after my arrival. She looked around the room and reviewed my chalkboard. She looked baffled and said, "Don't forget to put your objective on the board." I was clueless, but I agreed. Obviously, it was something that I was supposed to know how to do. Mrs. Scottie returned another day during the same week; the objective was not on the board. Then she realized that I did not know how to write an instructional objective.

"Mrs. Artson, come to my office after school," she said sternly.

"Yes, of course," I replied with a smile.

I arrived immediately after school. Mrs. Scottie explained all the parts that the objective must contain and how to state it in behavioral terms. She quickly reviewed the curriculum and the textbook and briefly explained how grammar was taught in Baltimore City Public Schools. "Be sure that you do not teach grammar in isolation," she said firmly. I remembered the English coordinator who interviewed me saying the same thing.

The system's idea of grammatical instruction was very confusing to me, because when I was in school, back in the Dark Ages, teachers taught grammar in isolation and students learned grammar. However, during the 1970s in Baltimore City Public Schools, grammar had to be taught in context along with literature and writing. Teachers were not allowed to refer to the parts of speech by names: noun, pronoun, adjective, etc. That was the hardest thing for me to grasp. The students had no knowledge of the rules of grammar and usage, nor did they have knowledge of correct sentence structure or language mechanics. It didn't make sense to me to do it the system's way, but I was required to do it as directed. The system did not care what I thought, and the students didn't care about the method. They weren't interested in learning anything. They just wanted to play and have a good time.

The students thought Mrs. Artson's classroom was a playground, and they were delighted to come to the playground every day to talk, laugh, and giggle, to tussle around on the floor, throw paper balls at each other, scream, yell, and do whatever they wanted to do. For days, I stood at the front of the room, looked at the students, and wondered what in the world was going on. *Something*, I thought, *is very wrong here, because this is not the way school is supposed to be. This I know.* I didn't know a lot about teaching, but I knew that much.

This brings me to my next problem: classroom management. I had difficulty with classroom management during the early part of my first year. I was the mother of five children, but my children did not behave as these students did. I tried to correct the behaviors, but I was doing a really poor job. I didn't know what to do when the students misbehaved or were rude to me. So anger and frustration became my natural responses to these situations. One reason for my anxiety was that I believed the administration was fully aware of my situation but had decided to do nothing to assist me. Further, I felt that I stuck out from the other teachers, because no one on my hall was having the problems I was experiencing.

I had observed that other teachers maintained order in their rooms, and I did not understand why I could not do the same. One day I decided that I would follow one of my classes to see how they behaved in other teachers' classes. I was free two periods a day: one for lunch and one for planning. I decided to follow my first period class during one of my free periods. I looked in on them in their social studies class. I was shocked to find them sitting quietly in class, doing their work. They weren't playing. They were not tussling. They were not throwing paper. They were sitting there doing what the teacher instructed them to do.

I asked myself, *What's wrong with me? What's going on here?* I really thought there was something wrong with me. I was confused, so I spent a week observing my students in other classes. I found them always behaving appropriately. I was convinced by this time that I must be the problem.

After all, the students behaved properly for other teachers. I was the only teacher struggling to get their attention.

The more stressful the situation became, the angrier I became. There was no offer of assistance, and I was as mad as a hornet. I felt they'd just thrown me into the den to be destroyed by the lions. No one checked to see if I needed any assistance. It was as if they didn't care. Furthermore, I was starting to doubt myself. I wanted desperately to do better. So I studied the teachers who I'd observed with my students and decided to model them. Whatever I heard them say or saw them do, I begin to say and do. Well, it did not work. The students continued to laugh, play, throw paper, and have a great time at Mrs. Arston's playground. I regressed back to yelling at the students: "Sit down! Behave! Stop that! Do your work!" Of course, no work was being done because the students were not paying any attention to me. They were busy having a good time. They were rude, disrespectful, and arrogant. They ignored me, gave me hand gestures, rolled their eyes, and called me rude names. Additionally, they refused detention when I assigned it, which made me look weak and foolish.

By the end of my fourth week at the School of Hard Knocks, I was so exhausted that I truly felt like giving up. I remember a particular day after my last class left. I flopped down in the chair at my desk and put my head in my hands. I was on the verge of tears. I could feel them welling in my eyes. I felt hopeless and physically and emotionally drained from the constant effort to get the students to do the right thing. Recording my voice on tape would have been as effective, and I would not have exhausted myself saying, "Sit down. Be quiet. Do your work," over and over. I thought, *This is punishing, and I will not continue putting up with it. I'd rather sell peanuts in the market than go through this every day. Something has to change. Is this really the job for me? I cannot go home tired like this every day.* I had children at home who needed me, but I had no energy for them. I didn't have energy for anything. I knew that this was not the way it was supposed to be. I had a real dilemma. I was doing everything I knew to do, but nothing I tried worked with the students. I tried detention. The students refused detention. I tried enforcing the class rules. They paid no attention to class rules. I tried calling their homes; the parents cursed me. I grew more and more confused and discouraged. I really did not know what to do. Yet I knew that teaching worked because I saw teachers doing it, many of whom were enjoying it.

Out of pure frustration, I approached the principal for help. I don't know if I was more afraid of him or the situation in my classroom. I began talking to Mr. Eergel in a quiet and composed tone. The more I explained what I was going through with my classes, the more upset I grew, until I cried and trembled. He listened and handed me tissues while I'd poured out my heart.

He slowly and calmly said, "You just have to let the students know who is in charge. They're just testing you, and you're failing the test miserably. They are having fun at your expense. Just take charge of your classes. Let them know that you're the star of the show. Mrs. Artson, you must get control of your classes." He continued patiently, "You cannot teach in confusion. You've got to learn how to control your classes," he repeated.

He put his arm around my shoulder and led me to the door. He looked into my tear-stained face and said, "All new teachers go through this. You'll be all right. Just let them know who is in charge." I thought, *They know who's in charge; they are.* Nevertheless, I gave Mr. Eergel's advice a lot of thought. It made perfect sense. However, an important fact was missing. He didn't tell me how to take charge. He just told me to do it.

I'd heard Mr. Eergel speak about classroom management several times, and I'd heard from other teachers that classroom management was his pet peeve. I also knew that I would soon be observed by either Mr. Eergel or Mrs. Scottie, and I did not want to be embarrassed by having them see my classes in such chaos. I was miserable and wanted to quit; yet I wanted to prove to myself that I could overcome the obstacles and be successful. I was aware that often success does not come without cost. So I continued tirelessly to do my best to improve. Finally, I decided that if I was going to remain at the School of Hard Knocks I was really going to have to get help. Who better to ask for help concerning student behaviors than a psychologist?

One day when the school psychologist, Dr. Knight, came to visit our school, I went to his office to talk to him about what I was going through. I was very emotional, and I know that my frustration showed. I was shameless about it, because I had reached the point of quitting. In fact, I told him that I was so discouraged that I was seriously considering giving up. He told me not to give up. He agreed to come to each of my classes to observe and get an idea of what I was facing. He said that he'd get back to me with his thoughts on the matter. He could not visit all my classes in one day, but he would try to visit them all within two weeks. Dr. Knight was very positive and encouraging. He talked with me about my stress and gave me several suggestions to try, so that I could continue on the job until he had the information that he needed to help me. His advice was simple.

"Take time for yourself. Be sure to eat breakfast and lunch. Take time to relax. If possible, get out of the building during the day and walk around the block. Exercise is a good stress reliever. Most of all, know this—it's not you. It's your circumstance. You'll be all right. I'll help you."

I felt more encouraged than I had in a long time. Somehow, I knew I'd be okay. I left his office knowing in my heart that it really was not me. It was the situation. Most of all, I believed that I could be successful in the classroom.

Dr. Knight kept his word. The next day he arrived at my first period class before the students arrived. He wanted to observe them as they entered the room. The students did not know who he was, so they looked him over a couple times. For the most part, they ignored him. Dr. Knight sat in the back of the room and wrote copious notes. He did the same thing in my other classes, until he'd visited all of them. In every class the students gave him the onceover and then ignored him, and in every class the behavior was business as usual. I tried to get the students' attention. They did what they liked; however, I no longer felt hopeless because I now had an ally.

After Dr. Knight had visited all of my classes, he invited me to his office to discuss his findings. He did not sit behind his desk. He pulled up a chair close to me, so that we were facing each other. For a brief moment, he looked over his notes. He had taken very good notes and had perfect descriptions of the most disruptive students in each class. He had also noted what I did, what I said, and how the students responded.

"You are trying too hard," he said.

"I'm trying too hard?" I asked, puzzled.

"Yes, you are trying too hard to control another individual." He explained, "You are trying very hard to control the students. You cannot control another person. You can only hope to influence their behavior, but you cannot control the individual. For example, if Johnnie wants to throw a piece of paper across the room, he will throw it. What you do after he throws the paper will determine if he does it again"

I was confused by his statement, but I continued listening to his advice. He talked for a long time about my students' behaviors and my reactions to those behaviors.

Lesson Learned

Classroom management is a very crucial component in the classroom environment.

Word to the Wise

Anyone who is interested in the teaching profession, especially anyone who has not had teaching methods courses, experienced student teaching, or worked as a substitute teacher, should visit several schools at the level of their teaching interest: elementary, middle, or high school. Request to sit in on several classes, some in which classroom management is good and the teacher has control of the classroom environment and some in which the classroom management is not good and the teacher does not have control of the situation. This will allow you to observe the student behaviors that teachers deal with on a daily basis, providing insight so that a sensible decision about teaching can be made. It will also help to prevent the absolute and complete agony that I experienced during my first year. You will know what to expect.

As a prospective teacher, you will be able to make an intelligent decision as to whether teaching is for you, and you will avoid finding yourself standing in front of the class wondering, *What have I gotten myself into?*

I learned very early that teaching is not simply standing before the class and attempting to deliver instruction, nor are the students always overjoyed and excited about being taught. Teachers can get the students interested in learning. However, it doesn't come automatically. No fairy comes to the class daily to sprinkle goobie dust over the students, causing them to behave in the appropriate manner or making them do what needs to be done so that they can learn. Therefore, the prospective teacher needs to know that classroom management is an essential component in teaching and must be mastered quickly.

Classroom management is vital to teaching. This is why I sought help with my problem. It is a known fact that teachers cannot teach in confusion and students do not learn in chaos. I continued working with Dr. Knight. He was helpful in pointing out that my problem at the time was primarily trying to control the students as opposed to trying to influence their behavior. Over time, he gave me a list of strategies to practice, which helped me learn to influence student behavior. Dr. Knight also advocated the use of rewards as opposed to punishment. He scheduled several strategy sessions with me.

During the first session, we discussed detention. I told him that the students would not come for detention. We looked through the handbook to find the procedures for dealing with students who refused detention and discovered three steps to follow. The first was to remind the student of the detention. If the student still refused detention, contact the parent. If the student continued to refuse detention, the third and final step was to report the matter to the principal. That was good news, because I'd seen Mr. Eergel in action dealing with disruptive students, and I knew that he was not a pushover.

Dr. Knight also taught me the appropriate way to assign detention. He told me to stop yelling at the students.

"Purchase a few packages of bright yellow chalk. At the first sign of disruption, go to the chalkboard and write the word *detention* and the number one under it. Once you have identified the culprit, get the student's attention, direct his or her eyes to the board, and write his or her name there."

I thought for a moment "That's it?" I said, frowning in disbelief.

"Yes." He said, "Don't make a big fuss about it. Near the end of the period, simply place a detention notice on the student's desk. Don't say anything, just place the notice on the desk. It is the student's decision to obey or disobey the rule. You must remember that you cannot control the student. What he or she does about the detention notice is up to him or her. Simply follow this strategy and the procedures in the handbook."

"My students will refuse," I said.

"That's where you come in. You cannot make the student come for detention, but you can influence his or her decision the next time that detention is assigned."

He referred me to the handbook. We reviewed the school procedures again.

"Just follow the school's procedures. It will probably take time for the students to realize that they can't win the detention issue, but it will be worth the wait."

He said I should remain calm and patient and allow the procedure to work and that I should not deviate from the procedures. I tried the strategy. It didn't give immediate relief. However, after a few weeks of referring students to parents and to the principal, it worked. The day finally came when all I had to do was write the word *detention* followed by the number one in bright yellow on the board and the class immediately came to order. The students finally realized that there was a definite consequence for misbehavior in my class. Yippee!

It worked! It really worked! For weeks, I'd been telling students all day, "I need to see you after school today," and giving them a detention notice to return. They paid no attention to me. In fact, many times I found the detention notices in my wastepaper basket. However, the word *detention* and the number one written on the board in bright yellow chalk worked. Order had been established with a piece of bright yellow chalk and a calm, confident teacher.

Another of Dr. Knight's helpful strategies was to have the students develop the class rules and the consequences for infractions. I continued to use this strategy throughout my teaching years. The thought behind this strategy is that if the rules are theirs, they have buy-in and will more readily adhere to them. With that in mind, the students in each class and I developed rules and the consequences for breaking the rules. I grouped the rules and consequences from each class and combined them into one set of rules for all classes. The students really liked the strategy. If students broke a rule and didn't want the consequence, I'd remind them that they had made the rules and the consequences. It worked beautifully.

Dr. Knight taught me to be unafraid, particularly of things that were beyond my control to fix, and how to examine expectations to determine whether they were realistic or unrealistic, pragmatic or impractical. He also helped me to understand that school administrators and supervisors are typically very demanding in their expectations, which are very often unrealistic.

"You will go home feeling stressed many days if you try to fulfill all the expectations of other people," he said.

He really helped build my self-confidence, which allowed me to realize that I could do anything that I set my mind to do, if I believed in myself. He taught me how to better understand the students and the strengths and weaknesses in their personalities.

"You have instilled in your children the values that you want them to have. The students are not your children. They come to you from various homes and with different values. You cannot force your values on them nor expect them to behave as your children behave. However, you can influence their behavior through the use of various strategies."

I was extremely grateful for Dr. Knight's help. The environment in my classroom soon became appropriate. However, I continued to have issues with the curriculum, which did not meet the needs of my students. It was one size fits all. Most of my students were underachievers. The main problem with the curriculum was that it lacked the appropriate skill levels to meet the wide range of student abilities in my classes. As a new teacher, I didn't know how to group students for the best instructional and learning benefit. Fortunately, I learned these things later.

However, during my first year this lack was an issue. Sad to say, not one of the supervisors found it necessary to teach me how to work through such situations. I suppose the intent was that I should teach myself. In fact, that's exactly what I did. With the help of Mrs. Charity and Mrs. Kinder, who were both special education teachers, I learned to teach the underachievers. What was interesting was that although I was concerned about teaching, my students were not concerned about learning. The students did not want to work. Their lack of work ethics and effort were big problems. I believed that teaching worked, and I had developed a genuine interest in student achievement. The more often students displayed a lack of interest in learning, the more bothered I became. I was fully aware of their frustrations about the lessons, and I knew also that something had to be done to stimulate their interests. Yet I did not know what to do. I spoke with Mrs. Scottie about the situation. She said, "Just follow the curriculum."

Lesson Learned

New teacher syndrome is caused by a lack of professional training as well as a lack of administrative and supervisory support.

The good news is that although I was striving to overcome curriculum issues, I had defeated the classroom management fiend. I had established good rapport with my students. I had established an effective classroom environment and had connected with parents. These three important essentials are needed for successful teaching.

I'd been working with Mrs. Kinder and Mrs. Charity for a few weeks before it was time for my first classroom observation. Mrs. Scotties told me that she would be in to conduct an informal observation on Monday of the following week. I did not know what that meant. I asked Mrs. Kinder. She told me that the department head would come to one of my classes and sit there the entire period to observe my instruction. *Oh, God, I'm in trouble now,* I thought. I had no idea what Mrs. Scottie was expecting, but I did know that I was still having trouble making the curriculum work for my students.

Over the weekend, I carefully studied the curriculum to prepare for Monday's lesson. I included all of the components in the lesson plan, which I felt was probably in the correct form. However, I was concerned about the students' abilities to meet the instructional objective with 70 percent accuracy, as required.

Monday morning arrived and found me extremely nervous. My heart beat forcibly against my chest, and I trembled noticeably. I didn't know which class Mrs. Scottie would visit, I just knew this was D-Day. I meditated and took some slow, deep breaths. Finally, I was able to relax and regain my composure.

It happened that Mrs. Scottie came to observe my last period class. I had just settled my students and started the drill when Mrs. Scottie arrived. Carrying a manila folder and a clipboard, she took a seat at the back of my classroom. Almost as soon as she was seated, she began looking around the room and taking notes. I tried not to focus on her but instead to concentrate on the students and the lesson at hand. I will never forget the lesson I taught that day.

The activities for the lesson came from the grammar book assigned to grade eight. However, my students had not mastered the concepts and did not obtain 70 percent on the assessment as required. Even though the class was orderly and the students participated well, Mrs. Scottie focused on the final activity, the assessment.

"Your students did not meet the objective. We'll talk about it tomorrow during your planning period," she said without a smile, and she quickly walked out of the room.

Her attitude during the conference the following day was cold and indifferent. "Your room looks very nice. However, you need to work on pacing the lesson. You spent too much time on this, that, and the other; the students did not meet the objective. Blah, blah, blah blah, blab blah." She offered no suggestions for making the lesson better.

I was hurt and confused. I just sat there and stared at her. I reminded her that I had spoken with her about the fact that the curriculum and materials were too difficult for my kids. However, she chose to ignore my explanations and said that I needed to learn to use the curriculum. I was very annoyed at her attitude when I left her office, because I had worked so hard trying to do all that was expected of me with little or no help. But I was also determined to win. I began to think of the entire observation procedure as a minor skirmish in which I knew I must triumph.

Soon after the observation conference came the Christmas holiday break. I was beginning to feel that even though I was improving, perhaps teaching really may not be for me, so I decided to use that time to make a decision as to whether to continue teaching. Were the unrealistic expectations and lack of support I received worth it to me? I saw the system I worked for as cold and the leadership Machiavellian. I knew the stress and continuous aggravation were not good for my well-being or my children's.

Over the Christmas holiday, I considered all that I had experienced and my abilities and limitations. I thought about Dr. Knight's counseling and the positive feedback I had received from him. I could hear his voice in my mind's ear saying, "Don't give up. You can do this." I smiled when I remembered a teacher who'd criticized me for having him in my class so often. She'd said, "Dr. Eergel is aware of this, and he is going to think that you're very weak if you need this much help."

I had struggled without help for so long that I was beyond worrying about what others thought. Suddenly I was filled with boldness and the determination to overcome all obstacles and to learn all I needed to learn in order to become an effective teacher. To become aware of the students' academic abilities, I planned to review their full academic records when school reopened. A glimmer of success appeared.

Reflecting on the problems my students were having, I decided to design a plan to stimulate their interest and to teach at the level of their abilities. The bored students were not learning and were talking too much at inappropriate times, which meant that I had to stop the lesson to get the students back on track. I was convinced that the talking was tied to the instruction. Consequently, I developed a new strategy to handle discipline problems, assess the students' abilities, and review their skill competencies, all using the same method. This unique method was later called the Artson Treatment. The Artson Treatment required a variety of resources and necessitated that I spend a great deal of my own money.

Teachers are ordinary people with
extraordinary determination and strength.

S. Artson

"Education is the constraining and directing of youth towards the right reason which the law affirms."

Plato

Two

I began teaching during the seventies, which seems like the Dark Ages now. At that time, schools used ditto machines and duplicating sheets to make copies. The top sheet of the duplicating sheet was white. This was where an activity was written. The second sheet was coated in a special type of ink in purple, blue, or red. When the activity was written on the white side of the paper, it picked up the color of the ink on the attached sheet.

The several ditto machines in school were usually broken, or else no paper was available. I could not trust that the machines would be in working order or that paper would be available when I needed it. Knowing this, I purchased a used ditto machine, several gallons of fluid, a box of ditto sheets, and three cases of plain white copy paper. Teachers could also purchase pre-printed ditto sheets in books of skill activities, so next I went to the teachers' resource store and looked for ditto books offering activities from basic to advanced skills. The pre-printed activities typed on perforated ditto pages could be used many times.

I spent several hours in the teachers' resource store looking for materials appropriate for the wide range of abilities in my classes, including grammar and mechanics, on three levels: basic and intermediate skills, plus a few on the advanced level. I also looked for books that covered the reading skills in the curriculum. Although my students were eighth graders, all of the books I selected were at fifth- and sixth-grade levels, because my students could not handle materials on the eighth-grade level. I made sure that all the books I chose contained skills that matched the curriculum.

In addition to time and money spent purchasing books and materials, the Artson Treatment also required a great deal of preparation time. I had to plan the lessons, as well as duplicate and collate the materials. I studied the curriculum and selected the materials for the first five days of school. To begin my new strategy, I wrote lesson plans that included grammar usage and mechanics, reading comprehension, vocabulary, and writing, and developed a diagnostic test. I also developed a new seating chart for each class. I seated those students with the worst behavior problems in the front of the room next to students who I knew would not talk to them.

When I returned to school after the Christmas break, I was more confident, assertive, and positive and much more fit for the job. When I had started at the School of Hard Knocks in September, I had been apprehensive and afraid. However, this was a new beginning. I was now familiar with the curriculum, and, with the appropriate materials, I was now prepared to teach it. Furthermore, I knew my students. I knew which ones were going to try to give me trouble and which would not.

My return was invigorating. I came back to school refreshed, with renewed energy and zeal. I knew in my heart that I was not a quitter. I had never walked away from a challenge, and I was not going to walk away from this one. Nor was I going to allow anyone to drive me away. I had begun to see my situation as it was: a challenge, a test of my true strength. I was not going to fail the test again. I believed that I would have regrets for the rest of my life if I did not see this through. I had decided to put myself on a timeline. I would do my very best for the remainder of my first year; then I would reassess. I was comfortable with my decision. It felt as right as rain.

The first day of the Artson Treatment turned out to be a very interesting day. The only difficulty was establishing the new seating charts. I'd written the students' names on index cards and taped the cards to the desks where I wanted students to sit. Seating directions were written on the board in bright orange chalk. It directed the students to find their names on the desks and to sit in that particular seat. When hall duty was over, I entered the room and found the students mulling around looking for their names and complaining about not being able to sit where they wanted. I went to the chalkboard and wrote the word *detention* and the number one under it on the board in bright yellow chalk. One student noticed what I'd done and alerted the other students.

Finally, everybody noticed that I'd written detention on the board. They whined about not being able to find their seats but calmed down. I said, "You can find your seat, if you stop talking and look for it." It took another two to three minutes for everyone to find his or her seat. The same situation occurred at the beginning of each class that day.

I went over the instructional objective, which indicated that they would take a diagnostic test. I heard more murmuring. Most students did not like their seat change and did not want to take a test. Therefore, they put up a little fuss. I explained that it was a diagnostic test and the results would not count against them. In each class, it took most of the period for the students to complete the tests. I then informed the classes that I would be using a new strategy for the next few weeks, and they should come to class prepared for a change the next day.

That night I graded the tests. The results gave me the opportunity to clearly see for the first time my students' abilities in the areas tested. Most of the students did poorly on the test. The results helped me to determine how to best use the materials I'd purchased to achieve the best benefits for the students. After I analyzed the results, I was ready to fully execute my new strategy, which consisted of a daily learning packet containing the instructional objective, the drill, the skill activities, the homework, and the daily assessment. I created a learning packet for each student in preparation for beginning the new strategy the next day.

The second day I stood at the door and greeted each student in my period one class. I felt good because I could now call each by name. I gave a learning packet to each student who entered the room and said, "The directions are on the board. I'll be in after hall duty." Everyone took a packet, looked at it, and took a seat, but they were very noisy and playful.

When I entered the classroom, I found pandemonium. The students were not seated. They were standing around laughing and talking. *Oh no,*

I thought. *They've lost their minds, or they think that I have lost mine*. I knew that my students had chosen to forget the positive classroom environment that we'd worked together to establish prior to the break. Sometimes old habits die hard. As a reminder, I went to the board, selected a piece of bright yellow chalk, and wrote the word *detention* and the number one under it. Then I flicked the lights off and on a few times to get the attention of the class, and I directed their eyes to the detention board. Immediately they overcame their selective amnesia and settled down.

I directed their attention to the instructional objective board and explained the strategy that we would be using for a few weeks and the reason for the change in lesson format. Next, I directed their attention to the drill, class work, and homework boards. On the drill section of the board, I had written the drill directions and the phrase (contained in the packet). I did the same for the class work and home assignment. I explained that the same directions were in the packet they'd received. I also asked the students to open their packets so that we could go over the format.

I stated, "I will only explain this one time, so you will have to pay attention in order to know what to do. The first page of the packet is a list of instructions for working through the packet. The next page is the drill. Complete it and raise your hand when you are finished. As usual, you have five minutes to complete the drill. The next four pages are the class activity pages, and the last page of the packet is your homework. Tear it off, write *Homework* and the date, and place it in the homework section of your notebook. You must complete the entire packet in order to get a good grade. I will return the packets to you tomorrow."

One student in my first period class said in a loud voice, "What's this sh-t? I ain't doing all this work."

Another student said, "She must be crazy. I ain't doin it neither."

My response was, "That's your choice."

After I was sure that the students understood my directions, I told them to begin. As I walked around the room observing what students were doing, I noticed that most students were working very hard to complete the assignment. Once the students started doing the work, they realized that it was not constructive busy work. It was actually a review and I was obviously serious about them completing it.

My classes for the remainder of the day were about the same. A few students in each class complained and spoke out against my new strategy, and a few students chose not to do the work. Some students put their heads on the desks and closed their eyes. I told them it was their decision whether to do the work or not, but they could not put their heads on the desks. They did not like my comment, but complied. A few students refused to do the work. I told them to write their names and the date on the first sheet. I did not allow their lack of participation to discourage me. I had a plan, and I was going to work my plan. I continued to walk around the classroom observing what students were doing and to provide assistance where needed. I did not sit during any of the instructional periods.

The students' desks were arranged in rows so that I could easily walk up one row and down the other. I took off my heels, put them in my closet, and replaced them with a pair of comfortable flat shoes so that my feet would not hurt as I walked up and down the aisles. Close monitoring allowed me to clearly observe which students were working and which ones were not. One of the things that I learned early is that teachers need to be physically involved in instruction.

I wanted to continue this teaching strategy. However, it required a lot of work. I spent no less than four to five hours every night preparing for the next day: grading the packets, recording the grades, writing the lesson plan, running more copies for the next day's packets, and stapling the packets together. I returned each student's graded packet the next day, including the incomplete ones. I knew that immediate feedback was the key to the strategy.

I decided that I would definitely continue the strategy. It worked like a charm. Most students in my classes completed the work and assessments grades were improving. The students were always anxious to see how well they'd done. The few students who refused to do the work in the beginning finally decided to join the others. I also started using stickers. All students received a sticker. I used sad face stickers for those who were not doing their best. I also called their parents. Gradually, they decided to work harder because they too became grade-conscious.

The students' assessments revealed that the Artson Treatment was working. It was fantastic! The activities held students' interests, provided a good review, and helped establish and maintain order. Students did not have time to play. Most of all, it allowed me a better grasp on my students' academic strengths and weaknesses. I was able to get a genuine sense of my students' abilities. However, it really was a tremendous amount of work on my part.

Although everything was coming together nicely in my classes, I must say that there were times when I truly wondered how much longer I could continue using the strategy. Keeping up with all the paper grading was exhausting. Despite the awesome amount of work involved, it was well worth the result. I continued the

Artson Treatment for six weeks. Once it ended, I repeated the diagnostic test that students had taken at the beginning of the strategy. I was very anxious to see how much the students had gained. I was more than pleased to find that 90 percent of my students passed the test with 85 percent accuracy or better. It was obvious to me that the students were ready for the assigned curriculum in modified form. I was also ready; I had learned how to make materials fit the abilities and interests of my student.

The students worked diligently. As a result, they gained confidence in their abilities. I could now use some of the required texts, along with the ancillary materials. What's more, most of the students took me seriously as a teacher. Therefore, I was able to correct the misbehaviors that occurred in the classroom with little effort and meet the needs of students on various skill levels. Finally, I felt comfortable in my role as teacher.

Lesson Learned

Appropriate strategies are the catalyst to launch effective instruction.

Although the strategy I used required a great deal of work, the value was immeasurable. Consequently, it solved my problems by strengthening my students' self-confidence and stimulating their interest in learning. The Artson Treatment only works if students receive immediate feedback. My belief regarding student work is that it must be graded and returned to students within two days; any longer and it loses its meaning and purpose. In my case, I had forty students per class. That meant grading approximately two hundred learning packets every night.

I don't want to paint a picture that everything was perfect every day. It was not. I had one student, Jerry, who was the last to decide to do the learning packets. That's not bad when you consider that he was only one out of the two hundred students assigned to my classes. However, he was adamant that he was not going to do the work. Jerry would come to class, place his packet on his desk, and put his head down. He would not sit up; he would not do the work. I tried different strategies to encourage him to comply. I called his home and talked with his mother about his refusal to do the work. She said that she would talk with him. Still he refused. I checked with the guidance counselor about his behavior. His counselor said that he was being stubborn. Finally, I kept him after school to talk with him about the importance of doing the work.

"Jerry, if you do not begin to do the work, you are going to fail this quarter."

"I don't care. It's stupid. Just fail me. I don't care. I ain't doin' your dumb work," he said in a nonchalant manner.

"Do you understand the assignments, or do you need help with the work, Jerry?"

"No, I don't need no help. And anyway, you ain't teaching me nuffin'.."

"I'm trying to find out what you're able to do and what your interests are. The packets help me to do that," I said.

"I don't care. I ain't doin' it," he shouted.

He remained determined that he was not going to do the work. He did not consider what I was doing to be teaching, and he was just not going to the work.

The time arrived to send out deficiency notices: reports sent to parents of students who are in danger of failing a subject in a particular quarter. Most of my students did not receive a deficiency notice. However, Jerry did. When I gave him the notice, he looked at it, balled it up tight, and threw it in the trashcan. I suggested that he might want to get it out of the trash and take it home, or he would be meeting with Mr. Eergel in the morning. So he took it out of the trash, shoved it in his back pocket, and left the classroom.

Lesson Learned

I cannot control my students. I can only hope to influence their behavior.

Jerry decided to take the deficiency notice home because there was a serious consequence for his refusal to do so. When he came to school the next day, he was willing to give the learning packets a try. His mother's comment on the return portion of the deficiency notice was, "Jerry will do as he is told. Call me if he does not." Jerry started doing his work and life was sweet again. It is my belief that consistency is a primary virtue in the classroom. Perseverance works.

It took a while to achieve full participation in the Artson Treatment and to get the students to realize that I was very serious about their involvement in their own learning. However, it allowed me to move on and try something new. I taught myself to use groups for many activities. My students and I genuinely enjoyed working together. They loved working in groups because it gave them the opportunity to share ideas and help each other. Grouping also helped me better assess their achievement. I learned that if the work was too difficult for them, the result would be frustration, and that would ultimately lead to misbehavior. I sat down with all groups, assisted where needed, and kept the students on task. It was marvelous. I was now sharing with my family at home how great it was to work with these kids. The environment in the classroom had improved tremendously. I very seldom had to write *detention* on the board. All I had to do was just look at the blank detention board and students complied. They knew the consequences for misbehavior in Mrs. Artson's class.

I spent time with students after school, sometimes so that they could complete unfinished work, sometimes for coach class, and a few times for detention. During the 1970s, it was an accepted rule to keep students after school for various reasons. However, teachers today have to practically make an appointment with students and their parents to detain them after school. It's ludicrous and serves no purpose to detain a student two or three weeks after an offense has occurred or to wait two or three weeks for an appointment to provide needed assistance to students. During the seventies, that was not the case. Teachers simply let the office know that a student was being detained, and the office notified the parent. My students were well aware of the consequence for not returning to my class when directed to do so.

In February, I realized that I was fully content in my role as classroom teacher. I was no longer going home exhausted from yelling all day or upset because the students would not comply. Though I was going home with many papers to grade, I was overjoyed because I really felt that I was doing a good job for kids. Nonetheless, it had taken me a long time to get there. Through my determination to win, I was finally able to succeed.

An additional point worth noting is that except for Mrs. Charity and Mrs. Kinder, I did not have any colleagues with whom I related. Teachers, for the most part, left me on my own. They offered neither assistance nor criticism. I did not want to wear out my welcome with Mrs. Charity and Mrs. Kinder. Therefore, I spent most of my school day in my classroom. At first, I felt isolated and disunited from the other teachers. However, later I was so focused on improving my teaching skills that I appreciated the time. In fact, I started using my lunch and planning time to grade papers, call parents, or peruse materials for instruction.

I was pleased with my professional growth. My students and I had a mutual understanding. I was there to teach, and they were there to learn. Good rapport is an outstanding benefit in the classroom. When students see the teacher as a fair person, they will more readily give respect; they will work harder and they will accept correction and helpful criticism. It is not necessary that students love the teacher, but it is imperative that they are respectful and that a good working relationship exists. I believe that I learned this quickly because it was essential. The rapport with parents was so good that they gave me permission to physically discipline their children.

One time in particular, I was having problems with a disruptive male student. I called his mother to discuss his classroom conduct, and she came to see me about the problem. I explained his behavior in detail and showed her his work folder. She became even more concerned.

"Mrs. Artson," she said, "the reason that you're having a problem with Mike is because all you do is talk. He only understands one thing and that's a whipping. I am giving you my permission to wear him out."

"No, thank you," I said. "If you want your son whipped, you'll have to do that yourself. They do not pay me to beat children. Furthermore, I am too old and too tired to beat children. I will talk with Mike. I will punish him, but I will not whip him. If whipping him is something that you think must be done in order for him to pay attention in class, you will have to do it yourself."

"All right then," she said. "I'm just telling you that you have my permission to do what you need to do, and you won't have a problem out of me if he comes home and tells me that you beat his butt."

I simply said, "If he comes home and tells you that I beat him, it will not be the truth. I do not have any intention of whipping your child, or anyone else's child, for that matter."

The good thing about this situation was that the parent trusted me to discipline her child in such a manner. However, I was not so naive not to see what may have also been behind her request. If I beat him, she would not have to. I had only been at the school six months and a parent was telling me that I needed to physically discipline her son and was giving me permission to do it. I was wise enough to realize that physical punishment should not come from the teacher. Working in concert with parents is good, but the parent's recommendation that I beat her child was not.

Meanwhile, the end of the first six months of the school year approached, and I was experiencing a sense of accomplishment. I now had a system for doing most things. A sense of unity existed in my classes. The students and I had reached an understanding. You might say we had sort of a quid pro quo relationship. They understood their role as students, and I understood my role as teacher—or so I thought.

"Education does not mean teaching [students] to know what they do not know, it means teaching them to behave as they do not behave."

Ruskin

Three

One afternoon I was in my classroom preparing for the next day. The students had left for the day, and the building was quiet and peaceful. I'd turned on my radio and was listening to quiet music while I organized my things and prepared to leave. I put some things in my briefcase and hummed to the radio, unaware that a student had entered the room until he cleared his throat. I turned in the direction of the sound and saw Damien standing there. He was one of my overage students; seventeen years old, average height, and average weight.

I was startled, but I turned to face him and said, "Yes, Damien, what can I do for you?" He stood there for a moment staring at me. Finally, he spoke.

"Ya know, Mrs. Artson, you really cute."

I was shocked. That certainly was unexpected.

"Damien, that is inappropriate. What do you want?"

"Just wanna talk to you."

I checked to make sure that my door was open; it was. I knew that Mrs. Kinder and Mrs. Charity were in their rooms across the hall. I wasn't worried, but I was very uncomfortable.

Damien was doing his best to give me a come-hither look that he'd probably seen in the movies. He slowly walked over to where I was standing, looking me up and down all the while. His bogus attempt at being charming was working on my nerves and I thought, *Enough of this nonsense.*

"Damien, you need to leave now," I repeated. He tried being more provocative, getting that certain look in his eyes.

"Don't you like me, Mrs. Artson?" he said softly.

I'd had it with his *Gone with the Wind* theatrics.

"Look, boy, you are going to leave this room right now, before you say or do something that you're likely to regret for the rest of your life. I mean it! Never approach me in this manner again! Do you hear me?" I shouted.

He just gave me what he must have considered an alluring smile and left the room. I immediately went across the hall to Mrs. Charity's room and told her what had occurred. She told me to report the incident to Mr. Eergel. I did so the next morning. Mr. Eergel handled the matter promptly, but Damien continued to give me his version of come-hither. I realized that I did not have the power to change his facial expressions. However, he was really annoying me. I did not find Damien's behavior flattering.

I decided to talk with Dr. Knight about the situation. He told me that Damien's behavior was a means of distraction and intimidation. He said that I should use it to get him to work harder. I did not have a clue as to what he meant by that, nor how to accomplish it. Dr. Knight said that he'd stop by for a visit to observe Damien.

I also went to the guidance counselor to get background information on Damien. I found that he was three years behind and had a history of poor attendance. He'd also spent time in juvenile services. I was aware of his academic ability in English because I'd tested all of my students. I also knew that he was failing my class. After Dr. Knight observed Damien's behavior, we developed strategies to draw him into the lessons. I started calling on him to answer questions and had the class respond to his answers. I also put him in a group that would nudge him to participate and would give him kudos for his group participation.

Finally, Damien became interested in learning, and the inappropriate behavior diminished. He started studying; he knew that I would call on him to answer questions. He began volunteering to answer questions and was anxious to participate. He also became interested in a girl in the class who reciprocated his interest.

By the middle of March, all of my classes had come together in total support of each other and of me. However, there are no perfect classes, because there are no perfect students and no perfect teachers. Nonetheless, I had mastered the art of classroom management to the extent that I could simply raise an eyebrow or say *"Students"* in a firm but low tone, and the class would come to order. I was proud of myself, proud of my students, and proud of the accomplishments that we'd made. I'd made it very clear to them that they would respect me and I would respect them. I'd stressed that it was much more important that we respect each other than it was for us to like each other. Fondness, I believed, would be the natural result.

Nevertheless, I still had a few students who were problems from time to time. One day a student was transferred to one of my classes. Her name was Livel Moned. She made it clear that she did not like our rules or the consequences for breaking them. It was also very apparent that she was not interested in anything but creating confusion. Therefore, she gravitated toward the few students in the class who were still not completely compliant to the class rules. I could tell from the very beginning that she was a troublemaker. She was a ruffian, very boisterous and antagonistic.

The first day in class, her behavior was confrontational and obnoxious. Fortunately, most of my students were not impressed with her antics. She was defiant and hostile and somewhat of a bully. Consequently, I decided to visit her guidance counselor to get some information about her history. I was informed that she had been removed from her previous class because she did not get along with the teacher, who was a veteran teacher of several years. That bothered me. I was a first-year teacher, and I'd worked strenuously to establish myself with my students. Now I had been given a real problem. I felt put upon; betrayed. I thought, *If a veteran teacher couldn't handle her, why was she assigned to my class?*

I went to visit Dr. Knight and asked him to observe her behavior. He was somewhat knowledgeable of her history and also did not understand why she had been placed in my class. He agreed to visit my class to observe her behavior a few times and then meet with me to discuss his findings. When we met, he said that she definitely had authority issues. Dr. Knight suggested that I check to see if Livel was a special education student who'd fallen through the cracks. He also recommended that I test her and keep a log of her behaviors and that I should not change my classroom strategies when working with her. She would have to comply.

I spoke with Mrs. Greene, the special education department head. Mrs. Greene said she was familiar with

Livel and had scheduled her to be tested, but the tests would not be done until April. Then the committee would have to meet with the parents. All of these things would have to be done before Livel could be placed in special education if the test results indicated that she needed the change. In the meantime, I would have to deal with her behavior. I was given a form and told I should document her classroom behavior on it.

I was really angry to know that the school would assign this student to a new teacher. Next, I went to see the eighth-grade assistant principal, Mr. Moodi Paine. He was unpleasant and arrogant, as usual. His response to my concern was indifference.

"Well, what do you want me to do? She had to go somewhere; why not your class?"

I reminded him that I was a new teacher and not trained to teach special education students.

"You'll have to deal with it. There's nothing I can do," he growled.

I stood there and stared at him for a couple of minutes. He just ignored me. Finally, I turned and walked away. I decided that I'd keep the log of her behaviors and continue to teach the class as usual.

A couple weeks later, Livel came to class in a very hateful mood. She tried starting arguments with a couple of students, refused to do her work, and was generally uncooperative. I picked up a piece of bright yellow chalk, went to the detention board, and wrote the word *detention* and the number one. A student noticed that I had written on the detention board and said, "Uh-oh." A few students looked at the board. The class had not seen me use this strategy for long time. When Livel heard the student's

"Uh-oh," she looked where the other students were staring and noticed the board.

Finally, she said, "What the hell's that 'pose to mean? You can put my name up there all you want. I ain't comin' to no damn detention." I did not respond to her comments but continued what I was doing. Near the end of the period, I completed a detention notice, indicating disrespect toward the teacher, using profanity in class, and disruptive behavior. I placed it on her desk. She got up from her seat, ripped the form, tossed it in the trashcan, looked at me, and laughed. Her new-found buddies in the class also laughed. I ignored her and continued to close my lesson. I added her buddies to the detention list on the board and also gave them notices.

Her buddies came to detention that afternoon, and I talked with them about their behavior, but Livel did not come. The next day I followed step two of the detention policy. I gave her another copy of the detention notice. She balled it up and threw it in the trash again. The third day I called her home. Her mother told me that she would speak with her. Livel still did not come for detention, and the matter was referred to Mr. Eergel the following morning. Sometime during that day, he sent for Livel and gave her a three-day suspension. She was to return with a parent the following Wednesday.

This made Livel very angry. After school that day, I went to the ladies room to wash my hands. When I tried to exit, the door was jammed. I pushed and pushed as hard as I could, but I could not open the door. Then I heard giggling on the other side of the door. I yelled through door, "Move away from the door now!" Livel yelled back, "No, bi-ch. Stay your a - - in there all night!"

She and a group of her buddies were pressed against the outside of the door, and I could not get out. The girls continued pressing their bodies against the door. I could hear them laughing for some time. Finally, a teacher came up the hall to investigate the loud laughter. It was after school, and students should not have been in the hall. She threatened to get the principal, and the girls ran out of the building.

The teacher opened the door and saw that I was upset. "Are you okay? she asked, concerned.

"I'm fine." I said. "I'll handle the problem in the morning. Thank you." I went back to my room and wrote a report for Mr. Eergel.

The following morning I spoke with Mr. Eergel about the incident. I also told him that I had spoken with Mr. Paine about Livel and had asked him for help, but was denied. Mr. Eergel said that he would get the names of the other girls who were with Livel and handle the matter. He said they'd all be suspended. I was relieved that I did not have to deal with Livel for a few days.

Things quickly returned to normal in class, and the positive classroom climate returned. My students rallied around to support me. I continued to make myself available to them at times that were convenient. I wrote early passes for students who wanted help before school; I worked through my lunch period with students who wanted help; and I provided coach class one day a week after school. My goal was to increase their achievement. Consequently, it was important that I provide extra help for those who needed it. This also gave me a greater opportunity to get to know my students.

Lesson Learned

Teaching has not occurred if students have not learned.

Livel did not return to school for a week. When she did, Mr. Eergel had her proposed for suspension. She was directed to remain at home until she received her new school assignment. It is good to count your blessings when things are going well, because there is always the chance that things will change without notice.

I will never forget the worst incident that I encountered that year. It occurred just before Easter break. The weather was great, and all was well with my five classes. We were looking forward to spring break. However, all of a sudden my fourth-period class started breaking class rules. Students came late to class, arrived making a lot of noise, and were very playful.

The class remained out of order for a few days. I was not at all happy about the change in behavior. I told the students that if they did not stop they would all have to come after school or suffer the consequences. They fully understood what that meant. They calmed down and order resumed.

Then one afternoon the students had just started the drill when Mattie got out of her seat and walked to the front of the room. She had a test paper in her hand.

"I need to talk to you 'bout this paper. You need to change this grade," she demanded.

"Have a seat. The grade is correct. I will not change it, but I'll be glad to go over the test with you and show you where you made mistakes, so that you can get a better grade next time. I'll see you after school," I said.

"Like hell," she said. "I don't want you to show me nuffin'. All you need to do is change the damn grade," she repeated.

"I'll talk with you after school."

"You gonna talk to me right now!" she yelled.

"No, I am not," I said, enunciating every word slowly and firmly. "I'll discuss it with you after school."

Mattie was furious. She balled the paper into a tight ball and threw it across the room toward the trashcan. It fell on the floor; she turned and walked away.

"Okay, then, it's gonna be your a-- after school."

I walked to where she was seated and asked calmly, "What did you say?"

She looked up at me with as much hatred as one can muster in a single stare and said curtly, "You heard me. I be waitin' for you out front after school." Then she threw her head back in an arrogant manner and laughed.

One of the strategies that I'd learned was to defuse arguments with students by remaining calm. So I decided to ignore her and continued the lesson. Mattie sat and pouted the remainder of the period. As she was leaving the class, she stood at the door and gave me a long threatening stare.

It made me very uneasy. I am four feet ten inches tall; at that time, I weighed one hundred and fifteen pounds. The student was approximately five feet seven inches tall and weighed about one hundred and forty pounds. I knew her friends who would encourage her to attack me and who would also help her. I asked the teacher next door to listen out for my next class for a moment, and I went to see Mr. Paine about the student's threat.

Mr. Paine laughed and said, "That girl is not going to bother you."

I told him that I was concerned and that I take all threats seriously. He continued to laugh and told me to go back to class, that I had no reason to worry. I looked him directly in his face.

"If the students attack me, I will defend myself."

"If you strike the students, you will be arrested," he said, laughing.

"Well, call the police now, because if Mattie and her friends attack me, I definitely will fight back. I will not allow these children to beat me. I just won't do that."

He laughed again and said, "You're making too much of this. You're making a big deal out of nothing." I left his office and returned to class.

The closer it got to the end of the last period, the more uneasy I felt. My heart raced like an engine in a high performance car speeding around the track in the Indianapolis 500. I knew that Mattie was quite capable of attacking me, especially with help and encouragement from her friends. Alone, on her own, she probably would not bother me. However, with and for an audience, I believed it was quite possible.

I prepared to leave school for the day. I slowly packed my briefcase, took my coat out of the closet, and put it on. I threw my purse strap over my shoulder, took a pair of sharp scissors out of my desk drawer and put them in my pocket. I was very upset at the thought of having to defend myself in this manner, but I was truly concerned for my safety. I was very disturbed because I knew that I had allowed the student to intimidate me. Moreover, I truly did not want to harm a child. So I approached Mr. Paine again.

"I really wish that you would look into this matter."

"Go on home. Those kids aren't going to bother you," he said nonchalantly and laughed.

I left his office and boldly walked out the front door of the school. Know this: Fear will make you bold. The adrenalin flows, and you suddenly become very courageous, as I was when I opened the front door.

I opened the front door and stepped assuredly onto the wide landing. Mattie and her buddies stood on the sidewalk in front of the landing, blocking my path from the building to the street. I pushed my shoulders back, held my head up, and kept my right hand on the scissors in my pocket. I looked Mattie directly in the eye. She wore a sinister smile. My demeanor was calm, relaxed, and assertive.

As I passed through the crowd, I was unruffled. I coolly said, "Pardon me." The students parted so that I could walk through. I stood on the curb with my back to the group, waiting to get across the street, my hand still on the scissors in my pocket. My car was parked across the street from the school. When the traffic cleared, I slowly crossed. As I approached my car, I took out my keys. I paused to ensure that I did not rush, and then I put my key in the lock, stepped in, and sat behind the wheel. As I pulled away, I heard the girls laughing at Mattie, calling her a chump. They taunted her because she'd backed down.

That evening, in the safety of my home, I reflected on what occurred. It made me feel uncomfortable to realize that I was capable of hurting a student with a weapon. However, in my mind, the students were going to hurt me, the school would not help me, and I certainly was not going to allow the students to beat me. This was a very tough school, and my fears were well founded. Of course, I was greatly relieved that I was not forced to use the weapon. Fortunately, the students hadn't known what I carried in my pocket or what I intended to do with it. I am grateful to this day that I did not have to use it.

The news of my courageous act quickly spread. However, at the time of the incident, I was concerned about my personal safety, and the fear of being beaten by students overrode my common sense. I could have stayed in the building and out-waited the students, but the next day I would have faced the same situation. The students would have thought that I was afraid.

Know this: When students think that you are afraid of them, they try to keep you that way. Therefore, the only thing I believed I could do was to meet the situation head on. I have never experienced another situation like that. I have worked with many difficult students, but thank God, I never had a student threaten me again. I have never feared for my safety as I did on that particular day.

The next day, I returned to school. Mattie came to class, sat in her assigned seat, and did not say anything about what had occurred the previous day. In fact, she was well behaved that day. A couple of the girls snickered at her when she entered the room. They were trying to upset her. My only comments were, "Calm down. Let's begin our lesson for the day." I taught the lesson as if the previous day had never happened. The best thing was that I felt a new inner strength. I was very calm and peaceful. I wrote an incident report for the principal, but I left out the comment about the scissors.

I spoke with Mr. Eergel later that morning, informing him that I had asked for help from the assistant principal and that I was afraid that I was really going to be forced to physically defend myself against students who seemed bent on hurting me. He waited until the end of the day, called for Mattie and her buddies, and dealt with the situation.

He told them, "Students do not threaten teachers in my school. If that's the way you're going to behave, you will not be allowed to stay here." He also told them that I could have brought charges against them for making the threat. He put a little of fear in the students. In addition, he suspended all the girls for three days and scheduled conferences with their parents. The issue was resolved. Mr. Eergel apologized to me for having to go through the situation alone. He reprimanded Mr. Paine for not handling the matter appropriately.

One thing I learned from that awful experience is that you cannot teach students who you are afraid of. nor can you teach in an environment in which you are afraid. Anyone interested in working with students must be bold and unafraid. Further, teachers need support from administrators who will come to their aid in cases of emergency. Teachers also need to support each other, because no one knows what may occur on any given day.

After the incident with Mattie, the environment in period four returned to pleasant and positive. It remained that way, except for an occasional flare-up by a few students. I handled those incidents in a calm, firm, and positive manner. When school opened after the Easter break, my students practiced the skills that they would need for the upcoming tests required by the school system. I offered several incentives for students who did their best on the test and for perfect attendance on test days. All was well in room 140.

Just when I thought everything was lovely and I had it made, I was faced with yet another predicament. It was near the end of the school year. My second-period class had been out of order for a few days. They were late coming to class and much too playful. One day I announced to the class that I would keep them through their lunch period the next day if they came to class in the same rambunctious manner.

Evidently, they did not believe me, because the next day they came to class in the same boisterous manner I'd complained about. I reminded them of the 60 percent rule. I had never used the rule. Obviously, the class did not think that I would, because they continued in their playful, disorderly manner. For some reason they couldn't pull themselves together. I don't know why they couldn't; maybe it was the warm weather.

The 60 percent rule states that when 60 percent of a class is disruptive and refuses to correct the behavior, the entire class receives the penalty. This helps to enforce the idea that the class is one unit. The 40 percent who are not misbehaving do not want to be punished. Therefore, they will usually put pressure on the 60 percent who are acting out. This was one of the agreed upon class rules and consequences. However, on this particular day, The 40 percent who were not misbehaving were enjoying the antics of the 60 percent who were. The chaos continued the entire period. Consequently, five minutes before the lunch bell was scheduled to ring, I wrote *Class Lunch Detention Today* on the board.

When the students noticed the announcement on the detention board, they tried to pull their act together, but I said, "It's too late now. You have had fun during this entire period, so you will miss lunch today." The bell rang, and I directed the students to pack their books and sit quietly. I did not escort them to the cafeteria for lunch.

About fifteen minutes into the lunch period, a student came to my room to tell me that Mr. Paine said for me to bring the class to the cafeteria. I sent a message back saying that my class was not coming to lunch. Mr. Paine sent the student back. This time the student stood in my doorway and yelled, "Mr. Paine said you better bring those students down now!"

I sent back the same message. Mr. Paine came storming into my room. He did not say anything to me. He yelled at the students. "Line up and go to the cafeteria!" Of course, the students thought that they'd won a victory. As they left the room, some of them looked back at me and grinned with *na-na-na-na-na* expressions on their faces.

I was furious! I stomped around the room for a moment swearing to myself. I sat at my desk and stood up several times. Then I hastily packed my briefcase, ran up the steps to Mrs. Scottie's office, and told her what Mr. Paine had done and said I was leaving. She tried to calm me down, but I was too agitated. I rushed out of her office. "I'm not going to put up with this!" I shouted. Then I walked around the building in an attempt to regain my composure. I returned to my classroom to get my things so that I could leave. Mr. Eergel was there holding the next class. He said, "I have provided coverage for your class. Please come to the office so we can discuss what happened." I agreed and went with him to his office.

Once the door to his office closed, I fell apart. He gave me a box of tissues and time to collect my composure. When I recovered from my hysteria, I was able to fully explain what had happened. I also told him about several failed attempts to get help from Mr. Paine. I explained my purpose for holding the class and about the sixty percent rule. He liked the sixty percent rule but said that teachers were not allowed to refuse the students lunch unless prior arrangements had been made, including a letter to parents so that students could bring a bag lunch. He said he understood what I was trying to do and realized I had been unaware of the lunch policy.

Then he looked at me with concern and in a very stern voice asked, "Were you going to just walk out?"

I responded with a simple, "Yes."

"If the same situation occurs again, would you walk off the job?"

"Probably. I don't know."

This made him angry, and he preached a five-minute sermon about my responsibilities and the proper protocol to follow in similar situations.

The following day Mr. Eergel called me to his office for a meeting with Mr. Paine. When I arrived, Mr. Paine had a cocky attitude. He was sitting in a chair facing Mr. Eergel with his head held high, legs crossed, and completely confident. He just knew that Mr. Eergel was going to reprimand me in his presence and that he would gladly gloat. To my surprise, Mr. Eergel supported me.

He began in a solemn tone. "Mr. Paine, Mrs. Artson is a new teacher and she is new to our school. I expect you to support our new teachers, not to humiliate and embarrass them in front of their students. You failed to do so. Your behavior yesterday may have diminished Mrs. Artson's authority with her students. She has worked very hard to establish order in her classes. The way you handled the situation yesterday was inappropriate."

Mr. Paine tried to defend his position, but Mr. Eergel simply held up his hand in the stop gesture and continued. "You have failed to support her in other situations when she asked you for help."

He then excused me to return to my class, saying that he would resolve the issue. Two weeks later Mr. Paine was transferred to another school. As it turned out, there had been problems with other teachers and Mr. Paine also.

Lesson Learned

It is very important to value your own self-worth and to stand by your own convictions.

Another trying situation during my first year included numerous pesky observations of my instruction. I was observed by administrators and supervisors a total of eight times that year: four informal observations and four formal observations. In addition, there were several classroom visits by specialists from the central office. I was observed so much that I felt like a lighted billboard on display in Times Square.

I was terrified during the first formal observation. The only thing that I was confident about during that observation was that I had established good rapport with my students by then and knew that they would do whatever they could to make me look good. Classroom observations were new to me, but not to my students. However, I was very comfortable with my last observation. By that time,

I knew what the observers wanted. They really wanted a show. They wanted me to pull out my bag of tricks and show them how well I worked with kids, show them how well I knew the curriculum. They did not want to be bored with the show. They wanted me to wow them. I had learned how to do that by the final observation.

As difficult as the beginning of the year had been, at the end of the year I was comfortable. Furthermore, I gave a post-test of the skills that the students had worked to master during the year and most of my kids showed impressive gains. Although they did not reach their appropriate grade level, they moved closer to it, and I was more than pleased.

Mr. Eergel was also pleased. So I was invited back for the next school year and was informed that I would have a full seventh-grade schedule. I gladly accepted the opportunity to return. I felt great about my progress and believed that I was quite capable of doing the job. I was as proud as a peacock. I danced around the room as I shared my good news with Mrs. Charity and Mrs. Kinder.

"The real object of education is to give children resources that will endure as life endures."

Sydney Smith

Four

I was greatly relieved when the school year ended, so happy that I felt like jumping up and clicking my heels together. Although I had learned a great deal during the ten months, it had been a stressful year. However, I liked teaching and wanted to continue to grow in the profession. With that in mind, I did a lot of soul-searching during the summer. I reflected on my first year as honestly and objectively as I could: the good, the bad, and the ugly. I thought about the mistakes I'd made and the lack of support that I received. I'd been told that I would have seventh graders the next year. To prepare for the year, I studied books on the scope and sequence of seventh-grade English instruction and books that dealt with the maturity and behaviors of seventh graders.

I was convinced that the second year would be much better than the first year. I could only surmise that during the first year I had been tested by fire and found worthy. I had proven that I could teach and manage student behavior and that I could establish and maintain a classroom environment conducive to learning. Therefore, I was assigned the top five seventh-grade classes my second year at the School of Hard Knocks.

Furthermore, I decided to take the necessary college courses to get my certification as an English teacher. I knew I would learn more about teaching and learning. Also, certified teachers made thousands more than I did as a provisional teacher. I needed to earn more money. However, this meant that I would have to get a loan to pay for the courses. So I spent part of the summer applying for school loans and registering for fall classes. I accomplished what I set out to do.

I had a wonderful summer with my children. However, I was excited about the new school year and anxious to begin. I arrived at the building two weeks prior to the opening of school, as Mrs. Charity had suggested. My new classroom was on the lower level. Mrs. Glad was the seventh-grade assistant principal. I'd noticed her the previous year and had heard that she was a very nice person and supported her teachers. This made me happy. I went to her office, introduced myself, and asked for the keys to my classroom.

There were a few of us in the building setting up our classrooms. We worked several hours a day until our rooms were complete and ready for students.

The room was clean, but I had much to do. I cleaned the desks, boards, and shelves with a disinfectant cleaner and arranged the student desks in a single row pattern for the first month of school. I knew that I could learn students' names quickly if they were seated in alphabetical order in single rows. I prepared my bulletin boards and set up places for learning stations. When my room was finished, I stood in the doorway and examined my work. I was as pleased as punch.

I practically leaped up the stairs to Mrs. Charity's room. I was excited, beaming with an ear-to-ear grin. "Come see my room," I said. She got right up, went next door to Mrs. Kinder, and invited her to come with us to see my room. They entered the room and were quite surprised. They grinned too.

"You've got it!" Mrs. Kinder said.

"It really looks nice." Mrs. Charity smiled, and she added, "We taught you well." They made no suggestions for improvements. We sat in the room and talked about how we'd spent our summer. Shortly after, they returned to their rooms. I stayed in the room for a long time, checking to see if I'd done all that needed to be done before I gathered my curricular materials and left the room.

I used the next week to prepare for meeting my new students. I was determined to have a better year with my seventh graders. For one thing, I would have them from day one. Also, I now had experience, and I knew a little more. I studied the curriculum and planned lessons for the first week. Along with the preliminary first-day things that teachers need to cover, I planned to give a diagnostic test. When I finished with planning and preparation, I felt more than ready for my students.

The first school day of my second year was terrific. Jittery with excitement, I arrived to work early, wrote my work on the chalkboard, and placed name cards on the students' desks. I was prepared with all the things I needed: a seating chart, class procedures, a diagnostic test, the student biography form, the required school paperwork that needed to be completed by students, and the students' class schedule. I would develop the class rules and consequences with the students. What's more, I looked and felt like a real teacher. I sat at my desk, sipped my cup of coffee, and relaxed for a few moments.

Finally, teachers were called to come to the auditorium to escort their homeroom students to the classroom. Thirty students were assigned to my class. Once the names had been called, I escorted my students to my room. When we reached the room, I opened the door and told the students to line up around the wall. Then I told them how to find their seats.

They were a little antsy, but they did what I asked them to do without complaining. *How wonderful!* I thought. The little darlings were just out of elementary school, scared to death of the "big school"—babies compared to the overage eighth graders I had taught the previous year.

It did not take long to establish classroom order. We developed the class rules and the consequences for disobeying them. They had fun with the activity. I truly enjoyed my students but found that I had to change my teaching strategies and demeanor to meet their maturity and behaviors. I was now Mommie Artson, no longer the tyrant of eighth grade.

Many of the students had sing-song, whiny voices. In fact, Mike, a boy in my 701 class, would sing my name when he wanted my attention. He'd speak in a very slow sing-song voice: *"Miss Miss Miss Miss Arrrrrtson."* After several days of the serenade, I said, "Please stop singing my name. If you don't stop, I'm going to change it." The class laughed, and so did Mike. Most of the students repeated "Miss" several times and sang my name.

That was a great year. I had a very supportive assistant principal, and the teachers on the seventh-grade unit were very friendly. They had their cliques, but they were friendly toward me. I sat at my desk one morning and noticed that I felt a comfortable sense of belonging. I felt that I fit in. I thought, *It is truly amazing how much a teacher can grow in one year if genuinely committed to improving.*

For first-year teachers, the interest in improving is often there, but it is sometimes difficult to maintain, because many, many times, even today, new teachers are thrown into their new positions and not given adequate help or real support. However, they are expected to be productive. During my first year, I had often felt like I'd been thrown to the wolves and forgotten.

However, when I returned as a second-year teacher, I was stronger emotionally, mentally, and professionally. I was assertive and confident. I refer to my second year as a classroom teacher as my year of jubilee. It was my "By George, I've got it" year. It was a celebratory year. There were no problems that I couldn't easily handle. I knew where important people and things were located in the building. I also had a supportive assistant principal I knew I could go to for help if I needed it.

My students were very immature, and I had to learn the idiosyncrasies of seventh graders. They were fidgety and needed frequent breaks between activities and constant motivation to keep them on task. However, they were delightful to teach. They came to class on time, sat in their assigned seats, and, for the most part, did what I asked them to do. Everything was going great for me. Dr. Knight stopped by a couple of times to visit. He was very pleased with what he observed and complimented my progress. I had come into my own teaching style. I was settled and happy, and it showed in all I did.

There was a new teacher across the hall from my room who was experiencing many of the same struggles that I'd had the previous year. I felt very sad for her because I knew first-hand how awful it is to come to work every day and face the kinds of difficulties that she was dealing with daily. My heart went out to her, and I wanted to help.

I'd had the bottom eighth-grade classes the previous year; she now had the bottom seventh-grade classes. Many of her students were also overage repeaters with major behavior problems. Undisciplined and disruptive, they were giving the new teacher a very difficult time. Every day I'd hear her screaming at the students, "Stop! Sit down! Do your work! Be quiet!" This would be repeated throughout each instructional period all day. I could feel her pain and frustration, because I'd just been through the same agony only a few months prior.

The student body at the School of Hard Knocks was predominantly African American and very urban. Mrs. Pleasant was middle-class and Caucasian. She had returned to Baltimore County after living in Colorado for a number of years. Mrs. Pleasant was not new to teaching. However, she was new to urban education. She was unfamiliar with the African American culture: the idiosyncrasies, colloquial expressions, and gestures. She was not prejudiced against African Americans, but she was very confused and uncomfortable with the students' behaviors.

She'd taught in Baltimore many years prior to living in Colorado, but she'd never taught in the city. Nevertheless, when she returned to Baltimore, she decided to accept a teaching position in an urban school. Mrs. Pleasant was struggling to find success in an almost impossible situation. She was not receiving any real support or assistance from the supervisor, assistant principal, or principal. She was reluctant to send many students to the unit office for fear of being considered weak or incompetent. She was doing all she knew to do in this very trying situation. It was not lack of interest that kept her from being successful, but the hellish environment in which she found in herself every day. The lack of assistance and encouragement also hampered her success in the classroom. Mrs. Pleasant really did not know what to do about the disruptive students that had been assigned to her.

Every day her students came to her classroom to frolic and amuse themselves in what they obviously thought was a wonderful place to have fun. They appeared not to know they were in a classroom and expected to work and learn. So they would break-dance; spinning on their heads, on their backs, or in whatever positions they felt like spinning. Some of the students were confused about the proper use of the desks. So they took to dancing or sitting on them. Others were puzzled about the purpose of the room and thought they were in a casino, so they played card games and pitched pennies. Then there was the strange little boy who was not a member of the class but who would come to Mrs. Pleasant's third-period class every day and hide in the little closet under the wall counter.

Some of the students must have been confused about the location of the cafeteria or thought that Mrs. Pleasant's classroom was the snack bar. They ate chips and other snacks and drank juice and soda there. As evidenced by the trash they left behind, they obviously consumed quite a bit during the instructional period. The students danced, played games, yelled, and laughed the entire period. They did whatever they wanted to do. This was the environment in which Mrs. Pleasant worked daily. No one came to her rescue. No one even bothered to stop by to inquire about any needs that she may have had. Teachers in the hall would comment, but no one would help her. I am not sure if Mrs. Glad was fully aware of the problem. If she was, she did nothing to help.

Since I had been tossed to the lions the previous year and survived, I knew how to tame their wild and restless spirits. One afternoon after school was dismissed, I walked across the hall to Mrs. Pleasant's room to say hello and offer my help. I introduced myself. She was happy to meet me. She was also a loner at school and glad for the offer of friendship and support. She was overwhelmed from all the stress. She was a more than competent teacher; certified to teach English, French, and Spanish. Despite her extensive background, she was not prepared for the shock that she received as a teacher at the School of Hard Knocks. She was definitely suffering from the lion's den syndrome.

During the 1970s, student populations in Baltimore City Public Schools were racially separated. The populations were either majority white students or majority black students. However, schools were not considered segregated. Although the student populations were primarily the same race, teachers and other professionals assigned to schools were not. White teachers taught black students and black teachers taught white students. Both races taught students of other cultures. For this reason, teachers such as Mrs. Pleasant, who lacked knowledge of the idiosyncrasies and cultures as well as the socio-economic status of various race groups, often found it difficult to work with the students in their assigned schools.

Trudy Pleasant and I became fast friends. I became her mentor as well as her friend. I taught her the Artson Treatment and shared other strategies that I'd learned from Dr. Knight. She developed strong classroom management strategies, and her students were soon responding to her in positive manners. She was then able to employ her own teaching style and techniques. The classroom environment was much better, and she was no longer screaming at the students. Trudy and I ate lunch together daily and talked after school. I was her support and she was mine. We became best friends, and to this very day, we are still best friends.

Lesson Learned

Support and effort make success inevitable.

One afternoon I visited Trudy in her classroom, and we talked about school as usual. She shared an incident that had recently occurred in one of her classes.

"Things were going well in all my classes. However, as luck would have it, that changed, and the students became out of control again."

"What happened?" I prompted.

"I was at the board teaching a lesson and was away from my desk for a while. Unknown to me, some of the students put glue on my desk chair."

"When did this happen?" I asked.

"One day last week."

"Do you know which students were involved?"

"I do now."

"What happened?"

I was surprised that she had not told me about the incident. I guess she was a little embarrassed. Trudy paused a moment and then began to tell me about the incident.

"When I finished working at the board, I sat at my desk to check the roll. After a few moments, I attempted to get up from the chair and realized I was stuck to it. Then I noticed the faint smell of the glue and realized that the students had put glue on my chair. The students were giggling. I did not let on to the class that I was stuck; I continued with the lesson from a seated position. The bell rang, and I dismissed the class. Some of the students were whispering and laughing as they left the room. I tried to get up but could not. I was really stuck. I guess sitting in the glue for so long didn't help matters. I was so angry I yanked myself up as hard as I could. I bounded up out of the chair and pulled the badly worn faux leather from the seat with me. It stuck to the seat of my pants. I was so furious I wanted to throw back my head and scream! I was glad that it was an old chair with thin, cracked faux leather. If not I guess I'd still be sitting there," she said.

"What did you do then? Did you go after the students?"

"No. I was too embarrassed. I wanted to go home, but I had two more classes to teach. I tied my sweater around my waist and taught the rest of my classes."

"Glue on the teacher's chair is an old trick, you know," I said.

"Yes, but I never thought it would happen to me. Most of all," she said," I was extremely disappointed in the students, because they've come such a long way and have been doing so well."

"It's a small setback," I said. "They'll fall in step again."

Continuing her story, she said that Mr. Eergel came to her class after school that day and asked if she had something to tell him. She told him that she did not. He told her that he had students in his office who had confessed to gluing her to a chair.

"Oh, my God!" I said. "What did you say?"

"I said that I was surprised the students had confessed and that I'd planned to handle it myself. He said that he'd already handled it and that the next time something like happens, I should inform him."

"Well, it's over now. How are the students behaving?"

"They're back on track," she said. "This incident let me know that I can teach in any situation, and that I should always look before I sit."

"Well, it's over now. Just put it *behind* you." We both laughed at the pun. Her laughter let me know that she was well-prepared for the next situation.

Trudy continued to make progress with her students. We were both having a good year. Nonetheless, the school year did not end without the dreaded instructional observations, as in the previous year I was observed eight times: four informal and four formal. However, I didn't worry about being observed because I understood the observation game and knew how to play it. What was ironic was that often the observer was not knowledgeable in the subject area and did not fully understand the demands of the curriculum. What's more, I knew that I could impress observers with a good show. I decided that there must have been a rule against giving new teachers more than "satisfactory" on an observation, no matter how good the lesson. I was convinced of this; that's what all new teachers received the first few years.

Trudy and I were both aware of the observation game. We worked together and supported each other the entire year. She was observed as often as I was. I shared the observers' preferences with her. She survived the numerous observations and received the usual satisfactory rating. We both had a handle on how to prevail in the classroom and became very effective.

As a result, our students were learning and growing. I accomplished things with my students that I would never have attempted with my eighth graders. The students wanted to learn and were enthusiastic. They loved praise and responded well to incentives. The seventh graders were fun to work with, but they did not cherish homework. I heard so many excuses for not doing homework that I could have covered a wall of my classroom with them.

The most common excuses for not having home assignments:

- I forgot.

- I lost it.

- I forgot to take it home.

- I did it, but I left it home, honest.

- I left it on the bus.

- I was real sick last night.

- Somebody stole my notebook.

Most of my seventh-grade students had very good attendance, but occasionally they would miss time from school. When they did, I always asked the reason for the absence, and they always had good excuses.

I was enjoying the certification courses. I was glad that I had decided to go back to school. By the end of the school year, I had completed the fifteen credits that I needed to get my certification and decided to enroll in a graduate program at Johns Hopkins University. I knew this would require making adjustments at home. I discussed my plans with my children and they encouraged me to move forward.

My success and growth were unfaltering. At the end of the year, Mr. Eergel invited Trudy and me to return the following year. We were told that we would both remain in the seventh-grade unit. We accepted the opportunity. More than anything, what I recall most about my second year at the School of Hard Knocks is that it was the year I met my best friend, Trudy.

I had a marvelous summer with my children and prepared to return in the fall. I also began my graduate studies. Although I was very busy, I was much more relaxed than I had been the previous summer. When I returned to school for the third year, I received my teaching certificate and an increase in my salary. Other than that, the year was basically uneventful. It was business as usual. My second year with seventh grade was a very good year. Nothing spectacular or out of the ordinary occurred. I was given the top five classes again, which was wonderful. The year ended for me as it had begun—great!

Where education has been entirely neglected, or improperly managed, we see the worst passions ruling with uncontrolled and incessant sway.

S. Parr

"All who have meditated on the art of governing mankind have been convinced that the fate of empires depends on the education of our youth."

Aristotle

Five

The fourth year was quite different. I was assigned older students again, this time grade nine. I was assigned the bottom five classes. The ninth-grade class as a whole was much smaller than the seventh or eighth grade classes, because students often dropped out of school before reaching grade nine. There were only twelve ninth-grade homerooms, and classes were grouped according to academic ability and behavior history. Two of the twelve classes were "self-contained" special education classes. Five of the twelve classes were comprised of the top ninth graders. These students were on or above grade level. The final five classes consisted of the underachievers. Their averages were two to three years below grade level. Many were ninth-grade repeaters.

Three teachers were assigned to ninth-grade English. Mrs. Courtney Patience was the special education English teacher. Miss Pristine Praise was assigned the top five English classes, and I was assigned the repeaters and underachievers. I was not concerned about this level of students because I had experience teaching lower achieving students.

However, when I met my students for the first time, I realized my work was truly cut out for me. While I was escorting my homeroom class from the auditorium, I heard their filthy language. They cursed all the way to my classroom. Every other word was profanity. When we reached my classroom, I directed them to line up in the hall so that I could give them directions. I told them that their names were written on cards and taped to the desks; they should find their card and sit at that particular desk. Immediately, they showed me their ugly side with profanity and bad attitudes. A male student said, "We ain't no damn kids, you know. You got us standing here like we kids. The hell with this!"

I ignored his comment and continued directing students. I allowed five students at a time to enter the room and find their desks. When all students were seated, I checked the attendance according to my seating chart. I had arranged the desks in single rows and in alphabetical boy-girl order. I began the seating on the right side of the room, first row, first desk, and ended on the left side of the room, last row, first desk. The students were directed to raise their hand when I called their names, so that I could ensure that they were seated correctly.

A few students had not followed my directions but had moved to be near a friend. I asked them to take the name card that they'd removed, place it on the desk where it was originally placed, and have a seat there. This meant that the student sitting at that desk also had to move. Again, more cursing, sucking teeth, rolling eyes, and grumbling.

"F--k this sh-t. This woman's crazy. I ain't movin'. Oh Gawd, she treatin' us like we f--kin' kids. The hell with this sh-t."

I chose to ignore the profane language and comments. It took fifteen minutes longer to seat the students and settle the class than it had taken to seat and settle my seventh graders the previous year.

Lesson Learned

It is sometimes wiser to starve students' need to disrupt with silence, than it is to feed it with a response.

I stood at the front of the room and looked out over my class and thought, *Working with this group is not going to be an easy task.* However, I knew in my knower that I could and would annihilate the profanity beast and the bad attitude varmint and ultimately win the battle. Therefore, I smiled and continued the opening day activities. I'd created a few class rules, but I informed the class that we would develop others together, along with the consequences for offenses. Despite the profanity and bad attitudes, the period ended on a positive note.

The students in the classes that followed behaved in the same rude manner and with the same bad attitudes as my homeroom students. They were arrogant, undisciplined, and hankering for a fight. These were the kids that Miss Praise did not want and that I was assigned to teach. These were the kids that are often referred to as *throwaway kids*. The students were carbon copies of the eighth graders I'd taught four years prior when I first came to the School of Hard Knocks. They were the same; however, I was not the same.

Lesson Learned

Hooligans are just people without purpose and direction.

I found out later that Miss Praise had spent time during the summer perusing students' academic and behavior records and had selected the ones she wanted in her classes. She picked the honor students, those on the success roll and closest to the top as possible. Since she was always assigned the honor students, she was always allowed to do so. She selected students without discipline problems and students with perfect or near-perfect attendance. She handpicked the best of the best ninth graders.

Miss Pristine Praise, referred to as Miss Priss or the Princess by other teachers, was the principal's favorite. She was allowed to do whatever she wanted. All she had to do was to put on a pouty face, look sad, or shed a tear, and the principal gave her whatever she desired—or at least it appeared that way. On the other hand, I could cry, pout, shout, and pee; it made no difference. I was there to do a job and I was expected to do it, as were the other teachers in the school. Most teachers did not like Miss Praise for that reason.

She was allowed to select the kids she wanted in her classes, and the others were assigned to me. These were the students who had attendance problems, had been suspended for one reason or another, and who fought. These were the over-aged students with the filthy mouths, the repeaters who belonged in grades ten to twelve. These were students who'd been latch-key kids since elementary school. These were the kids who she left for me to teach. I had no choice in the matter. However, I grew as person and as a teacher through interacting with her rejects.

As a result of working with these students, I learned patience and tenacity. They weren't the easiest by far to teach, but they had the right to learn. However, I had to curtail their use of vulgar language and profanity immediately. To accomplish this, one day I did a full lesson in all of my classes on appropriate language for particular environments.

In each class, I asked a student to write all the expletives used during the instructional period on the board in red chalk and the students' names who'd used them in green chalk. I did not correct the students' language. I continued with the lesson and did not respond one way or the other. Ten minutes before the end of the period, I directed the students' attention to the board to view the street language and profanity used during the period. The students were shocked. One of the male students in my first period class said. "Damn! Oh no, we didn't say all that." I pointed to the students' names and expletives written on the board and said, "Oh yes, you did."

The class laughed. At that point I initiated the cuss cup rule. One of the class rules stated that if students used profanity in class, they must put a quarter in the cuss cup. It was a rule and consequence agreed upon by all the classes. I purchased a large red tumbler with a lid and asked one of my students to decorate it. He drew caricatures of students getting their mouths washed out by the teacher. A sign over the cup stated, *"If You Cuss, You Pay."* The money was used for class purposes. For example, I would buy loose-leaf paper, pens, pencils, and other supplies that students needed. I would also use the money for rewards: candy bars, gum, etc. The students loved the idea. Instead of sending students to the office or detaining them after school for swearing, it was handled with an agreed upon class rule. The students had a choice between the cup, an office referral, or detention. They always chose the cuss cup. One day a student asked if he could give me an IOU. We all laughed. That started a new policy. I would accept a written and dated IOU. It was only good for two days.

The profanity rule worked because students had buy-in and a choice. After a short time there was very little profanity used in my classes. One day Timothy, a student in my last period class, came in and placed a handful of change on my desk. I could see that he angry.

"What is this?" I asked.

"I'm mad, and I know I'm gonna cuss a lot today, so I'm paying in advance."

The class laughed, and so did I. However, after I got the class started I called Timothy aside and discussed his problem. He was angry about something that happened at lunch. He calmed down and collected the money that he'd placed on my desk. I had really connected with my students. On the few occasions that students forgot the rule and cursed, they would apologize, the class would laugh, and we would move on.

Lesson Learned

Students' use of expletives is a habit that can be broken with the appropriate motivation and encouragement.

Although my classes were large, I was managing very well. Rules were established. The consequences for infractions were agreed upon and understood. Things were not perfect because there are no perfect classes, but an environment that was conducive to learning existed.

One day I noticed that Miss Praise was in a blue mood. She told me that some of the students were giving her trouble. I guess that foreshadowed what would soon be coming my way. By mid-October, Miss Priss was becoming disenchanted with some of her handpicked kids. She realized that some of the students she had selected were ruffians who did not respond well to her teaching style. She asked the counselor to remove the students from her classes. Of course, they were added to mine.

At first, there were only one or two students, but quickly my classes became stuffed to the hilt with Miss Praise's students. The walls of my room were practically bulging. My class lists of forty-five soon became fifty to fifty-five. Miss Praise's class lists were now twenty-five to twenty-eight of the best ninth-grade students in the school, all the cream of the crop, so to speak.

I complained to the counselor who'd assigned the new students to my classes. She told me there was nothing that she could do. Therefore, I went to see the principal.

"Mr. Eergel, my classes have grown from forty-five to fifty-five in some cases."

"That doesn't sound right," he replied.

"Please stop by any of my classes and see for yourself. I have wall-to-wall kids. I have no room for more desks. In fact, some kids are sharing the same desk. Some are sitting on the heat cabinet, and there is no room in the aisle to walk. It's a safety violation and unhealthy. Please stop by soon."

I gave all the new students a copy of the class rules and procedures and assigned each a class buddy. I also arranged to meet with them either before or after school. Most chose before school.

Lesson Learned

One can work through any situation with organization, skill, and patience.

Although the room was as hot as a sauna and not every student had a desk, my classes were pleasant and productive. The students and I had established a bond, and we worked well together. There were just too many of them in the small classroom. Miss Praise soon realized that some of the students that she'd had removed from her rolls would probably be returned to her classes. She went to the guidance office and perused the academic records of my students. Her game plan was to select students from my original classes who did not have behavior or attendance problems. Ironically, even though my students were underachievers and had posed serious discipline problems in the past, most no longer had behavior issues. Miss Praise did not want the students that she'd had removed returned to her classes. If she had to have more students, she wanted the best of what I had in my original classes. When I found out what she was up to, I was absolutely livid. I went to see her after school one afternoon. I found her preparing for the next for day.

"What do you think you're doing?" I demanded.

"I'm sure I don't know what you're talking about," she said with a faint smile.

"I'm sure that you *do* know what I'm talking about. You are not going to get my kids. You're going to get the same kids back that you kicked out of your classes."

"We'll see," she said as she turned her back to me and continued what she had been doing.

I was furious. I wanted to slap her silly, but I decided that wouldn't help me defeat her attempt to take my students. Instead, I went to see Mr. Eergel. I was very agitated, but I regained and maintained my composure.

"Mr. Eergel, I don't know if you're aware that Miss Praise is looking through my students' records to find students who she may be interested in having in her classes. She does not want the students she had removed returned to her classes. She would like to select from my original class lists."

"Are you sure?" he wanted to know.

"Yes. I just spoke with her about it. I will be very upset if she is allowed to do that."

"Don't worry, Mrs. Artson; I'll take care of it. She can select from the students who were originally in her classes."

I thanked him and left the office. I was greatly relieved that Miss Praise did not win this one. Within a few days, I received new class lists. Most of Miss Praise's students were returned to her classes. She was not allowed to select the students who she wanted from my original class list. Neither Miss Praise nor the students were happy about the change. The students liked my classes and did not want to go back to her classes. Returning them to her created a problem because the students felt rejected by me. I explained that I could not keep them with me because it was a matter of safety codes, having to do with the size of the room. I invited them to stop by to visit me. They were disappointed but understood.

My classes settled quickly after the return of Miss Praise's students to her classes. We were on course working to meet our objectives. However, a male student in one of my classes couldn't seem to get with the program. His attendance was poor, as were his efforts. He was in serious danger of failing for the year. He'd failed two quarters, and we were in the third. I had a serious talk with him after school one day.

"Edgar," I said. "What is going on with you?"

"I don't know. I don't understand what's goin' on in class."

"You would if you came to school. Why are you absent so much?"

"Stuff," he said.

"What does that mean?"

He looked down at his feet and shrugged his shoulders.

"Just stuff; I guess," he said quietly.

We talked for about thirty minutes and made a deal. I promised that if he would come to school, do his best to complete the work, and allow me to coach him before school or during lunch, I would help him to pass the third quarter. I would also assign a class buddy to help him in class. He lived up to his end of the bargain. When the quarter ended, I gave him a low passing grade, but high enough so that if he continued to work hard, he'd be able to pass for the year. A couple of days after grades were submitted, Mr. Eergel came to see me.

"How did Edgar Broon manage to pass your class and fail all others?"

I felt good about my response. "Edgar has potential and has improved his poor work habits." I said.

"Mrs. Artson, you cannot grade potential. You can only grade what the student actually produces, not what he has the potential to do."

"Do I have to change the grade?" I asked.

"I'll let this one stand, but never do that again, okay?"

A simple yes was my response.

Edgar was excited when he received his third quarter report card. Although he'd failed all of his other classes, he was happy that he had passed English. We continued to work together, and he was able to pass English for the year. His attitude about learning had changed. He developed a can-do attitude. Although he did not pass his other classes for the year, his grades improved in all his classes.

Lesson Learned

Giving students hope and encouragement is the key to changing potential into success.

By January of the following year, I decided that I was ready for a new challenge. I wanted to transfer to high school. With that in mind, I stopped by the main office one afternoon to have a brief conference with Mr. Eergel. His secretary told me that he was in an important conference and could not be disturbed, so I made an appointment for the next day. The following morning I found a note in my mailbox confirming an appointment for 3:45 that afternoon. As I made way to Mr. Eergel's office, I had mixed feelings. I didn't want to offend him by asking to leave, but I wanted the transfer to high school.

He greeted me with a smile and a nod. "Mrs. Artson, what can I do for you?"

"I would like a transfer to high school."

"Is that right?"

"Yes, I feel that I am ready for a new challenge."

"Is that right?" he asked again flatly.

"Yes."

"Most teachers in junior high want high school. You've done well here. If you can teach here, you can teach anywhere. I have no problem with your decision, and I'll support it," he said with a smile.

"You will, really?" I asked with excitement.

"Teachers get to high school and think they're in heaven; they rarely leave. It's hard to get a transfer to high school, but I'll support your effort. See the secretary for the transfer form."

"Thank you," I said with a big smile.

When I left his office, I was exhilarated. I felt great, as if I could do anything I set my mind to do. I was sure that I'd grown professionally and as a person during my five years at the School of Hard Knocks. My growth was unfaltering and steadfast. I gave myself a well-deserved pat on the back for all the hard work I'd done and the obstacles I'd been able to overcome.

Lesson Learned

Fear can paralyze growth. Never be afraid to ask for what you want.

I quickly filled out the transfer form and returned it to Mr. Eergel. He wrote a very favorable letter of recommendation and told me to attach it to the form.

The rest of the year was great. I continued to work to the best of my ability. I truly wanted the transfer to high school, but I'd learned how to survive where I was and I was not unhappy. I just wanted a change. Many times during the last few weeks, I reflected on my experiences at the School of Hard Knocks. I remembered my first year as very difficult and sometimes overwhelming. However, I was somewhat grateful for the challenges.

I believe that when a teacher starts out in a school environment in which student discipline is not a problem and materials and necessary resources are readily available, if he or she is later transferred to another school where these things are problems, the teacher will find it very difficult to make the adjustment. However, when the teacher has been tested and tried in the fire as I had been, that teacher can adjust to almost any situation in any school. So I looked forward to the challenge with great enthusiasm; I felt prepared.

Finally, in early June I received a letter from the central office stating that my transfer request was granted. I was being transferred to a vocational high school. Ironically, it happened to be the same high school that my youngest son would be entering in the fall. I rushed to Mr. Eergel's office to give him my good news. He told me he knew; central office had also informed him. He congratulated me and gave me a hug. I was so happy that I felt light as a feather as I left his office, as if I were floating.

I spent my spare time sorting my personal items from things that belonged to the School. I gradually took my things home. I was very happy about the new assignment. One thing in my favor was that Baltimore City Public Schools was in the process of converting junior high schools to middle schools. That meant that high school would begin with grade nine. I'd had two years experience teaching grade nine. The ninth-grade curriculum in high school was a little different from the ninth-grade curriculum in junior high school. However, the maturity level of ninth graders was the same. Even so, I hoped that I would be assigned upper-level classes at my new school.

I continued to work with enthusiasm and kept a sense of humor. My year ended on a positive note. Before leaving the School of Hard Knocks, I went to visit Dr. Knight. I told him about my transfer and thanked him for the support he'd given me. He shook my hand and wished me well.

Eventually, it was the last day of the school year and my last day as teacher at the school where I'd begun my teaching career. It was a bitter-sweet experience. I was excited about the opportunity to teach on the high school level and sad to leave the place where I'd gotten my start and where I'd become very comfortable. I thanked Mrs. Charity and Mrs. Kinder for their support and gave them each a big hug. I said a special farewell to Mr. Eergel. He wished me good luck. I'll always remember him. He was tough as nails, but he had a soft side too. I learned so much from him about how to be an effective teacher and a good leader. My friend Trudy and I saw each other socially; we met for lunch every Saturday.

I felt a little awkward when I stepped out the door for the last time. I stood on the sidewalk and stared at the building for a long time before walking to my car. I said a silent good-bye to the School of Hard Knocks and drove home.

I had a wonderful summer with my kids. We went on vacation at the Host Inn in Pennsylvania. It was great. I was very relaxed. I'd asked my son how he felt about me teaching in the same school where he was a student. He was very comfortable with the idea.

*"It is by education I learn to do by choice,
what [others] do by the constraint of fear."*

Aristotle

Six

I was thrilled about the chance to teach high school. I was also anxious to begin. Two weeks before school was scheduled to open, I went to my new school to prepare my classroom for the opening of school as I had done at my previous school. When I arrived, I went directly to the main office to introduce myself and to get the keys to my classroom. I stood at the counter for five minutes before I was acknowledged by the office staff. One of the secretaries approached the counter. I greeted her with a broad grin, gave my name, and asked for the keys to my classroom. I explained that I wanted to get an early start preparing my room. The secretaries looked at each other with a *whoop-de-do* expression. They were very cold and indifferent and not at all impressed by my enthusiasm. I was given the keys to my room by one of the secretaries without further comment. When I asked the location of the room, she merely glanced and pointed in the general direction. I decided not to allow the attitudes of the office staff to put a damper on my day. The room was on the second floor. I climbed the steps of the nearest stairway and found my room.

When I opened the door to my classroom, I nearly fainted. It looked like a junk bomb had exploded in there.

The teacher's desk was covered with carelessly stacked old books, many falling apart. Books, folders, and papers had been tossed on the top of the metal cabinet that covered the heating unit. More books, papers, and folders were piled high on the wide window ledge that ran the length of the room. Books were piled high on shelves next to the heating unit; books were stacked on the floor along the walls; books and papers were stacked on some of the students' desks. There were piles of papers and other materials in various places on the floor. Rodent droppings were over, under, around, and between the books and papers. Rodent droppings were in corners of the room and across the piles of books and papers on the window ledge.

In addition, there was dust an inch thick everywhere. The students' desks were antiquated. They were the old wood type that had the deep metal book compartment under the desktop. Graffiti was carved deep into the wooden tops and colored in with black and blue ink. Additionally, very explicit sexual drawings were carved into some desktops, along with crude, profane language. The book compartments were filled with balls of paper, candy and gum wrappers, wads of chewing gum, and small bits of old cakes and chips. Gum was also stuck to the undersides of the desks. The chairs were also covered with graffiti and drawings of all kinds. There were no casters on the legs, and, therefore, when touched they rocked like a drunk. The chalkboards were filthy with graffiti in colored chalk. The ledge below the chalkboard had thick layers of chalk dust. In addition, graffiti covered the cork bulletin boards that were attached to two walls.

There were sticky black stains on the floor from something that had spilled and dried. I opened the closet door and jumped back as a huge pile of papers and rodent droppings exploded from inside the closet and fell at my feet. I was glad that I was quick to jump back when I did. Had I not, all the trash would have fallen on top of my head. The closet overflowed with old papers, old used folders, old paperback books, bags of junk, and bags of trash that had been stuffed in the closet.

Some of the papers were so old they had turned yellow along the edges. An old plastic pail was lined with black grime and filled with dirty, hard sponges and stiff, filthy rags. Rodent droppings were on all the shelves. The closet had a horrible musty smell. I left the door open because there was too much trash still in it and on the floor in front of it to close the door.

This was the condition of the classroom that I was assigned. I found a clean paper towel and brushed the dust off a chair, sat, looked around the room, and thought, *Oh my God. Why was this room assigned to anyone?* I dared not go to the main office and complain because I would have to deal with the indifferent attitudes of the secretaries, who would undoubtedly just shilly-shally over the matter. So I just sat in the dirty room for a moment and stared at the mess. The longer I sat and looked at the mess, the more bothered I became.

Finally, I went to the main office to voice my concerns. There was a secretary at the counter when I arrived. Once I was able to get her attention I said, "I don't know if you all are aware, but the room that I was assigned is in horrible condition; it's a filthy mess."

She looked at me in a cool, dispassionate manner for a moment.

"I don't have a thing to do with rooms or room assignments. You'll have to see the assistant principal who handles that, but I doubt that he'll do anything about it."

Wonderful, I thought. She gave me his name and told me where I might find him.

I left the office to locate the assistant principal. It was a huge building, and I didn't have a clue about how to find his location. By the time I found him, I was livid, but I forced my composure to return. I introduced myself to him and explained my concerns. He had a nonchalant attitude. He stared at me for a moment and finally responded.

"Well, that's your room, so it's your responsibility. The cleaning crew will be through in a couple of days. They'll do the floor, but the rest is up to you. They are not going to empty the desks or clean out the closet. You'll have to handle that; it's your room. Now, I'm sorry it was left in such a mess, but you'll have to get rid of whatever's in there that you don't want. It's your room."

"What about the antiquated students desks, can they be replaced?" I asked.

"No, we don't have any new desks. After the teachers have set up their rooms, there may be a few desks available."

"What about chairs?"

"Same story. None available."

"Is there a teacher's desk and chair around in better shape than what's in there now? It's broken, and the drawers are full of junk."

"No. I'll have someone look around, but I doubt it."

"What am I supposed to do? Am I supposed to work in that mess?"

"I guess you'll have to clean it. The floor will be cleaned and waxed; beyond that, whatever you want done you'll have to do it yourself. Sorry, but that's just the way it is."

I was furious and could not understand why I was assigned a room in such horrible condition. I was greatly disappointed, hurt, and humiliated. Obviously, the administration expected me to clean the room or work in the filth. I also knew that I couldn't work in that filth and that a positive classroom environment was essential to learning and instruction. I left for the day knowing that I would have to clean the room.

On the way out, I met one of the custodians. I told her that I would be moving into room 236 and asked her about the dirt and junk in the room.

"The man who was in there retired. He had been in there for years. He always kept it junky; let the kids do whatever they wanted to do. Yeah, I know it's a terrible mess," she said.

I knew the answer, but I thought I'd ask anyway. "Is it going to be cleared out and cleaned before school opens?"

"Well, the floor will be mopped, waxed, and buffed. That's about it."

"What about all the old papers, books, and trash?"

"I guess you'll have ta do it. I guess it'll be your job."

"My job?" I asked, still puzzled.

"You movin' in, your job. We don't clean out the junk, nor does the cleaning crew. But if you pile the trash in the hall by your door, I'll haul it away for you," she said, and she smiled as she turned to walk away.

I thanked her and continued walking toward the front door. She was the first person to smile at me since I'd been in the building. I was really upset about the situation. I was beginning to sense the flavor of the school and assumed that it was every man for himself and God for us all.

I realized quickly that there was no point in complaining further because no one was going to do anything to help the situation. I went home and called my best friend, Trudy, and shared my day with her. She offered to go with me the next day to help me clean the room. That evening I purchased work gloves, rubber gloves, goggles, disinfectant cleaner, sponges, thick plastic garbage bags, scrub brushes, scrub rags, a bucket, dust pan, broom, shower cap, and a few paper respirators. I did not want to breathe in the dirt and dust.

Trudy and I met at the school at ten o'clock the next morning. I wore jeans and an old sweatshirt. I carried a change of clothes for after the cleaning chore. We went directly to my classroom. When we entered the room, Trudy said without thinking, "Oh my goodness. What a mess. It's worse than I thought." She sat at the teacher's desk and looked around the room. She tried not to let me know how concerned she was, but her facial expression said it all. I shrugged my shoulders and looked at her, perplexed.

"What am I going to do with this mess?" I said, slowly shaking my head.

"Well, let's see," Trudy said with a faint smile. "I'm sure we can do something with it. The first thing is to clear out all the junk. I'd be glad to help," she said, glancing around the room.

"No, that's all right. Just keep my company."

I stepped into the hall and spotted the custodian who I'd met the day before. I introduced myself to her and apologized for not doing so the previous day.

"Oh, that's all right. I could see you were upset, and rightfully so."

"I need a few barrels so that I can start clearing out all the junk in the room."

"I'll be right back. It'll be okay. I know it looks bad, but it'll be all right. Just push the barrels in the hall when you're done. I'll empty them and bring them back to you."

I thanked her and went back in the room. I stood there for a few moments to decide where to begin. In preparation for handling the books and papers that were infested with rodent droppings, I placed a plastic shower cap on my head, put a respirator over my nose and mouth, plastic goggles on my eyes, and a pair of work gloves on my hands. Trudy sat and watched my slow transformation into a hazmat worker. I looked like a character in a science fiction movie. The custodian returned with three large barrels.

"Oh, by the way," she said, "my name is Patricia, but everybody round here calls me Pat."

I lined the barrels with the thick plastic bags that I'd purchased and began by picking up the papers and books that'd fallen out of the closet the previous day. Then I started pulling papers and books from the closet. I did not see any mice, for which I was grateful, but they'd left plenty of evidence that they'd been there. I was glad that I'd brought the protective gear.

When I pulled the first stack of papers from a shelf, mouse droppings, dirt, and dust seemed to come from everywhere. I looked at Trudy, who had by this time moved to the far side of the room. I offered her a respirator, but she declined. It took two barrels to clear all the trash out of the closet.

I pushed the barrels into the hall and started clearing the trash from the window ledge. Before I finished that, Pat was back with the two barrels that I'd pushed in the hall, plus three more. I looked around at the junk still in the room and knew that I needed the additional barrels. I was thankful that she'd thought to bring them. I filled the five barrels with as much as they could hold, and still there was more trash left in the room.

Although there was much more work to be done, I was exhausted and dirty. So I decided to quit for the day. I cleaned up and changed my clothes in the ladies' room. Then, Trudy and I left for the day. She said that she was tired just watching me work. We went to one of our favorite restaurants, and she treated me to a late lunch. She said that I'd earned it.

I returned the next day, put on my protective gear, and continued clearing out the remainder of the trash. When I entered the room, I noticed that Pat had pushed more barrels in the room for me. It took eight more large barrels to finish clearing the trash that remained in the room. In all, fifteen barrels were necessary to remove all of the trash.

Next, I got a bucket of hot water from the utility room and poured a good amount of the disinfectant cleaner into it. I thoroughly washed the shelves, the closet, the ledges, and the heater cabinet. I cleaned the chalkboard and ledge and wiped down the bulletin boards. I cleaned any and all places that my students or I might contact. I even pulled the bottom windows open and cleaned them inside and out. I used a total of six large sponges and an entire bottle of disinfectant cleaner, and I had to change the water numerous times. By the time I was through cleaning the room, I was dusty, dirty, and tired.

However, when I stood back and looked at the results of my labor I was satisfied. The room was clean, bright, and smelled fresh. I was very pleased, except for the old dilapidated furniture that was built during Methuselah's time. When Pat stopped by to see how I was doing, she marveled at how much better the room looked. I smiled and asked if was possible for me to get better desks and chairs.

"I told the principal that we need to get rid of these old desks. They are just trash collectors. I'll see if I can find you some other ones. Usually you have to wait til all the teachers come back and see if they have any that they don't want, but as hard as you worked, I'll look around and see what I can find. How many do you think you need?"

I was pleased and smiled. "I don't know how many students I'll have, but thirty-five should be enough."

She left, repeating that she would see what she could find. I was beginning to feel better about my situation. I sat at my desk, glanced around the room, and mentally planned my bulletin boards and seating arrangement. It was four o'clock when I left the building. I'd spent the entire day cleaning the room. The cleaning crew was scheduled to do the floors that evening, and I hoped that I'd get newer desks and chairs soon. I considered trying to clean the desktops, but there was no hope—the ink was embedded deeply and seemingly baked into the graffiti carvings in the desktops, and there were profanity and obscene drawings on the desks. So I gave up on the old desks and prayed that I'd get better ones.

The following day, I returned to the school to do my bulletin boards. The teacher's desk and chair and the ugly student desks and chairs were still there. However, they were stacked in the hall outside of my room. The cleaning crew had been there to clean the floor. It looked great! It was so shiny that I thought it was still wet. I touched it to be sure that it was dry before walking on it. I carefully prepared the bulletin boards and taped headings for lesson components to the chalkboards. When I was finished I stood back to study my work. The bulletin boards and chalkboard headings added to the room. I was standing at the front of the room admiring my work when I heard a cart in the hall. I held my breath in hopes that it was Pat with my new desks and chairs. I ran to the door and found Pat coming down the hall with a huge flatbed cart. There were sixteen student desks and chairs stacked on the cart.

"Ms. A, I've got you some desks and chairs, but you might want to clean them out here, so that you won't mess up your nice clean floor," Pat said with pride.

I grinned from ear to ear. She unloaded the desks and the chairs and then stacked some of the old ones on the cart and took them away. I thoroughly cleaned the desks and chairs and carried them into the room. Pat quickly returned with more desks.

When she delivered the last cart of student desks and chairs, she said, "I'm lookin' for a teacher's desk and chair for you. How long are you gonna be here today?"

"I'll be here as long as it takes."

"I'll see what I can do. Either way, I'll stop back."

"Thanks," I said.

After she left, I carried the clean desks and chairs into the room and arranged them in a single-row pattern. In all,

Pat had brought me thirty-eight student desks and chairs. My classroom was finally beginning to take shape. The appropriate atmosphere for learning was beginning to develop, due to a large extent to a custodian who was kind enough to help me. No one else who I'd spoken with about the dirty classroom dilemma offered any assistance.

Lesson Learned

One of the greatest allies for classroom teachers is the custodial staff.

I didn't go to the school the next day. I'd already spent several days there cleaning and setting up the room. Now the end of the week prior to the opening of the new school year was near, and I wanted to shop for instructional materials.

Friday was the last opportunity for classroom preparations. The following week was scheduled for training sessions, conferences, and meetings. I did not realize that I was in for a big surprise when I returned to my classroom.

When I opened the door to my classroom on Friday, I was truly surprised. A new teacher's desk and a leather chair in good condition had been placed at the front of the room. Pat had cleaned them both. She'd even put a new ink blotter in the center of the desk. I was very happy, and I immediately left the room to find Pat. I didn't have much money with me, but I wanted to do something nice for her. I wanted to make her as happy as she'd made me. I found her in one of storage rooms. I could not help myself; I ran to her and threw my arms around her. She was taken aback by my display of gratitude. I smiled.

"Thank you so much for all you've done to help me." I pressed a folded twenty-dollar bill into the palm of her hand. "Please take this and have lunch on me."

"Baby, you don't have to pay me. I was glad to help."

"Please take it," I said. "You don't know what it's meant to me to have your support."

"Okay. Thank you."

I returned to my room, grinning all the way down the hall. I was ecstatic, spilling over with joy. My room was finally complete and looked like a teacher's classroom should. It was clean, bright, and inviting. I felt well prepared to greet my new students. That's how I started at Greener Grasses High School. However, it was only the beginning.

*"What greater or better gift to the
State than to train up youth."*

Cicero

Seven

I'd done all that I could to prepare my classroom. However, I didn't have the curriculum and materials I needed to begin planning lessons. I'd heard that department heads were in the building, so I decided to stop by the English office to introduce myself to the department head and ask for a copy of the curriculum. Mr. Patrick Prose was the department head. When I entered the office, he was sitting at his desk. I introduced myself and extended my hand. He ignored my gesture and turned his back toward me. *What's his problem*, I wondered.

"Mr. Prose, my name is Shirley Artson. I'm a new teacher in your department. Would you please tell me the grade I'll be teaching and give me a copy of the curriculum and teacher's editions to the texts I'll be using?"

He slowly turned to face me and snarled, "Grades, not grade; you will have ninth- and twelfth-grade classes. I'll distribute instructional materials at the department meeting next week."

I was reluctant, but I pressed at bit, attempting to get the materials that I requested.

"Since I'm new to high school, I wanted to study the curriculum and familiarize myself with the reading materials," I admitted.

He repeated in a harsh tone, "You will get the materials during the department meeting next week along with everyone else."

I stood there for a moment staring at him. I realized we'd reached a stalemate. I knew pressing further would have been as productive as swimming in sand. I turned and walked out of his office. I could feel him glaring at my back as I walked away. I decided to go home and think about the situation. I knew that I could not plan lessons because I had no idea what the curriculum entailed. I decided to apply what I'd learned from my junior high school experience and find or create a diagnostic test for each student for the first day of school.

I was beginning to have bad feelings about my decision to accept the position at the school. Everything in me was screaming, *You've made a huge mistake coming to Greener Grasses High School.* However, I'd learned that I could do anything that I set my mind to do, and I knew that somehow I would be successful. It would not be easy, of course, but easy had not been my forte since I'd become a teacher.

I researched the skills and literature required for students in grades nine and twelve. I also studied the skill requirements for grade eleven, because that let me know what the seniors should have mastered. In addition, I reexamined the ninth-grade diagnostic test that I had used at the junior high school. Then, I purchased other materials that I needed to create the two diagnostic tests. It took some time, but I created a test for grade nine and a test for grade twelve. In addition, I developed an all-about-me writing assignment that would serve two purposes. It would allow me to identify students' writing problems and also allow me to get to know my students. I paid to have the tests and the writing assignment typed and duplicated.

I was now prepared for the first school day. It felt super to have overcome the second obstacle at my new school. I knew there would be others, but I was also sure, really sure, that I'd prevail in those instances too.

Lesson Learned

Self-confidence, diligence, and determination triumph over most of life's impediments.

I had a wonderful weekend with my children and mentally prepared for Monday, when I would meet the faculty and staff. Thus far, I'd only met an unfriendly administrator and the inhospitable office staff. I hoped that my perception of the working environment was incorrect. *One could hope,* I thought.

With that in mind, I arrived at school early Monday morning and went immediately to my classroom. Shortly after, I heard voices in the hall and knew that the teachers were arriving. I remained in my classroom. My door was open, and I could hear conversations in the hall, but no one approached my door.

Finally, at 8:30 an all-call announcement came, directing new and transfer teachers to the cafeteria for a brief meeting with administrators. There were five of us, one assigned to each MESS subject department; one was assigned to the business department.

The principal was a short man with gray hair and dry, ruddy skin that resembled old leather. He introduced himself as Mr. Peter Meane. The four assistant principals were introduced in grade-level order: Mr. Dave Kcirp, grade nine; Mr. Caesar Thorn, grade ten; Mr. Napoleon Sharpe, grade eleven; and Mrs. Precious Elbaima, grade twelve.

They all shared lackadaisical, blasé attitudes. They looked us over with sour expressions that read, *Uh huh, more of the same.* I was not alarmed. I'd experienced unpleasant demeanors the previous week. The other new teachers had not and were taken aback, a little astounded at the attitudes of the administrators. I just sat there and smiled, thinking to myself, *You haven't seen anything yet.*

The principal gave us a little information about the history of the school, and then each administrator gave a little speech. We were given a copy of the school's handbook, and the other teachers were given the keys to their classrooms. Mr. Kcirp made a corny joke about the fact that he'd met me earlier when I complained about the condition of my room. I smiled and the others laughed. At the end of the meeting, we were directed to see our respective department heads for copies of the curriculum and instructional materials.

I knew better than to ask Mr. Prose for anything. So I returned to my room to wait for the department meeting, scheduled for later in the morning. I didn't have anything to do, so I was a little bored. Finally, an announcement directing teachers to their respective department meetings came. The English meeting was held in a classroom on the first floor. When I arrived, most of the English teachers were sitting in little groups chatting. They glanced in my direction and continued their conversations. I sat in the middle of the room. It was a large department with eighteen teachers, including me. By the time Mr. Prose arrived, all teachers were present. He did not introduce me. He simply waved his hand in my direction and stated in a flat tone, "Mrs. Artson is joining our department." The teachers looked in my direction. Some smiled faintly and others did not.

Mr. Prose expressed disappointment in the previous year's Maryland State test scores. He told us the dates and locations of citywide meetings and distributed teachers' instructional schedules. We were then dismissed to prepare our classrooms. I raised my hand to ask a question about the required texts and the curriculum. He did not acknowledge my raised hand. It was obvious that I was being ignored, and I did not like it. I could feel my blood beginning to boil as I grew angrier by the minute. I sat there for a brief moment, studying him. He was tall, average weight, with gray hair. His demeanor was disdainful. He appeared snobbish. His manner was condescending and seemed to say, *See how wonderful I am* as he glided out of the room. I wanted to follow him to his office and tell him what I thought about his arrogant attitude. However, I was smart enough to realize that that was not a good idea.

Instead, I went back to my room to regain my composure and to decide the best way to handle the situation. I convinced myself that this too would pass. Since my room was complete, I decided to tour the building, which was very large and complete with numerous tech-shops and offices. It was like a visit to another planet. I was pleasant as I passed teachers in the halls. They were cold and indifferent, but I greeted them with a smile. In most instances, my cheerful smile was not returned. *What a barrel of cold fish,* I thought. *These people must hate their jobs; what does that say for the school?*

I was determined that I would be happy. I continued my tour, greeting people as I passed them in the hall. As I passed Mr. Brown's room, he stepped into the hall to say hello. I gave him a broad grin. He invited me in for a brief conversation while he worked.

"Mrs. Artson, these people can be very cold. Don't let it bother you. It's just the way they are. If there's anything that I can do for you, let me know," he said in a sincere tone.

"I'll be teaching grades nine and twelve. I asked Mr. Prose for a copy of the curriculum and the teacher's edition to the required texts. He didn't give me either but said I'll get it later."

He smiled a knowing smile. I quickly came to know that Mr. Brown was very intelligent, comfortable in his own skin, and somewhat militant. I liked him right away and was glad for his friendliness. He allowed me to peruse his copy of the ninth-grade English curriculum and gave me student copies of the grammar text and the literature text. He did not have any twelfth-grade materials. He also explained what the class numbers on my schedule meant.

It became crystal clear that I was once again low man on the totem pole. I had been assigned the ninth and twelfth graders who had the lowest state test scores and probably the worst behavior problems. However, Mr. Prose didn't know me. I was new to Greener Grasses High School, but I was not new to teaching. I was also accustomed to teaching underachievers. I had learned a thing or two about challenges at the School of Hard Knocks, and teaching the underachievers was not a problem for me. I heard Mr. Eergel's voice in my mind's ear: "Mrs. Artson, if you can teach here, you can teach anywhere." He was right!

Lesson Learned

One can grow stronger through life's most challenging moments.

I left Mr. Brown's room feeling very positive. I was glad that I'd taken time the previous weeks to prepare my room. It was apparent that there would not be much time to do it this week. Several meetings were scheduled over the course of the week: the guidance department, grade-level administrators, subject departments, and two citywide meetings. Since the next meeting was scheduled for that afternoon, I left the building for lunch. It felt great to take a break from stares and unfriendly attitudes.

Almost as soon as I returned, an announcement was made directing teachers to the cafeteria for a faculty meeting. The principal, Mr. Meane, began the meeting by introducing the new teachers to the faculty. The high voltage stares of the faculty were anything but welcoming. They looked at the new teachers with expressions that questioned our right to be there. Cliques were very noticeable, and we didn't seem to fit in any of them. We sat together and sort of formed our own group. I'd experienced this type of rejection before, and I had adapted and survived. The other new teachers were really bothered by the negative responses, but I was focused on the job at hand.

The principal's agenda included his expectations and goals for the school year, changes in programs, and student enrollment. I was interested in his comments because I was new to high school. However, the other teachers did not seem interested. They murmured and complained about all of the meetings they were compelled to attend and because they were not given ample time to prepare their rooms for the first day of school. They complained, but no one listened.

They were right to complain about the long meeting. It was ludicrous to hold teachers accountable for classroom prep and not allow them time to do the work. Regardless of the teachers' objections, the meeting lasted ninety minutes. After a while, I began to share their feelings. When that meeting finally ended, we were directed to meet with our department heads for an additional meeting.

I didn't want to attend another meeting any more than the other teachers, but I saw it as an opportunity to speak with Mr. Prose about a copy of the curriculum. I waited for the opportune moment to broach the subject. When I mentioned the curriculum, he became very infuriated. He turned red in the face and looked as if he might explode any minute.

Speaking very slowly between clinched teeth he said, "I told you that you'll get it later." I was alarmed by his obvious irritation but decided to avoid a clash with him. However, I was really concerned; school was opening for students the following week, and I needed the ding dang curriculum. It was apparent that he was going to have his way about the situation.

The meeting lasted an hour. I don't remember anything that was said because I sat there in a state of indignation the entire time. I know that my facial expression expressed annoyance. Finally, we were dismissed with a reminder about both the superintendent's citywide meeting for all instructional staff and the citywide English teachers' meeting.

The superintendent's meeting was the following day. It lasted an hour, during which Dr. Manual greeted us, stated his goals, welcomed us to a new school year, and wished us well. The citywide English meeting was that afternoon and consisted of two parts: a ninety-minute general session and several one-hour workshops. The day was very long, but interesting and helpful. I learned how the system approached high school English instruction, and I met several high school English teachers. Some were friendly, and most were just cordial. Fortunately, I met a veteran teacher who'd taught twelfth-grade English for several years. She shared some of the basic curriculum information that I needed to know in order to teach British literature, as well as the language and writing skills that I needed to teach at the beginning of the course. I was greatly relieved. That meeting was the last in the series scheduled for the week. I was happy that I had gained new information about what I was expected to teach.

In previous years, I'd learned the importance of being prepared for the first week of school. I was more than ready with those types of activities. I also knew that Mr. Prose would give me the materials that I needed when he jolly well pleased, and there was not a thing I could do about it. I sensed that he danced to the beat of his own drum and would only assist me when it pleased him. However, I was confident that I would find a way around the obstacles he posed. En route home from the meeting, I stopped by the teachers' resource store and purchased the materials that I needed, including materials to use for review while I waited for Mr. Prose to give me the curriculum materials I needed.

When I arrived home, I immediately began laying out the materials I'd purchased. Later, I went to the store and duplicated the appropriate number of review activities that

I would need for a week. By the time I finished, I was exhausted. I had pushed the limits of my energy. However, I'd planned a wonderful weekend with my children, and I found the energy to take them to the Maryland State Fair the next day. We had fun, and I relaxed after all of the long, boring meetings I'd attended.

*"The foundation of every state is
the education of its youth."*

Diogenes

Eight

When school opened I still didn't have a copy of the curriculum, but I was not distressed. I didn't feel defeated or bothered about it. I knew that life was a journey and that unpleasant people are part of life's encounters. Recently I'd noticed a sign in a store window that clearly described how I felt that first day. It said, "Don't just show up; arrive with attitude!" I had decided that I was not only going to report to school the first day, I would arrive! I was excited, determined, and confident.

I'd stopped to pick up a cup of coffee en route to school and arrived ninety minutes earlier than required. I signed the attendance register, checked my mailbox for the class lists, and went directly to my room. I sat for a moment, sipped my coffee, and collected my thoughts. Then I began writing my work on the board. Later, I went to the office. I needed to have copies of the class lists run. One of the secretaries told me that they did not run copies. However, she said that she'd do it for me this time. When I returned to my room, I finished my coffee. I felt really ready to meet my students.

Finally, at 8:30, teachers were summoned to the auditorium to collect their homeroom classes. I had a ninth-grade homeroom class for first period. As I led them through the halls and up the stairs toward my classroom; I couldn't help overhearing their comments. I immediately realized that I had a nice, but lively, bunch. When we reached my classroom, I opened the door and waved them into the room, directing them to each find their name on a card taped to a desk and to sit there quietly.

They did the opposite. They entered the room like gangbusters, talking, playing, and laughing. I studied the class for a moment and knew in my knower that they were not *bad* kids; however, they certainly were energetic and also somewhat rambunctious. I loved them instantly. I was able to accomplish most of the activities I had planned and made a mental note to immediately work on establishing class rules with them, beginning with how to enter the room.

My next two classes were seniors; I had one senior class before lunch and one immediately after lunch. I'd looked forward to meeting them. They entered the room a bit noisily, but they quickly settled. They were delightful; a little playful, but no more than expected on the first day back from summer vacation. They were not the brightest of the seniors in the school, but I believed that they were the best. We were able to cover all of the activities I'd planned for the day and had time for a bit of informal chit-chat. I thought, *Oh yes, it's going to be wonderful teaching high school.* My last two classes were ninth graders, repeats of the first class. They were high spirited, playful students. *Yes,* I thought, *this is going to be very challenging.*

Lesson Learned

Teachers can learn much about their students when first meeting them.

During the next four days, I emphasized the class rules that the students and I had developed and Artson's Rules, which dealt with the behaviors that I definitely would not tolerate. My seniors immediately understood the difference. However, the ninth graders took a little longer. On day six, I found it necessary to institute Artson's Rule for correctly entering the classroom for my ninth graders.

I locked the classroom door and stood beside it in the hall, waiting for my first class of ninth graders to arrive. The students came down the hall in a loud and boisterous manner, as had become their habit. *My work is certainly cut out for me,* I thought. I smiled as I watched the first student struggle to open the door. He pulled it and jiggled the doorknob. Finally, he looked at me, rather dumb-founded. "Mrs. Artson," he said. "I can't get the door opened."

I was so amused that it took great effort not to laugh; he was so serious. I looked at him for a quick moment. "Darlin'," I said, "I know the door won't open because I locked it. Stand here," I said, pointing to the wall along my classroom. I directed the other students to line up behind him, single file, facing me.

"Why?" the student asked, still puzzled. I did not answer but gave the class a few moments to settle and to get the idea. Then I switched into my take-charge mode.

"I don't like the way you guys have been entering my room. So for the next few days or longer, when you arrive you will quietly line up as you are now. When you're quiet and calm, I will let you enter the room one student at a time. You will go in and sit quietly in your assigned seat until the whole class has entered. The moment you start talking or laughing, you'll come back to the hall and we'll start again. Do you understand?

"Yes," the class said in unison.

"Let's practice now," I said.

I let one student in, then the next and the next. By the time the fifth student entered and took a seat, I heard loud talking and laughing. I stepped just inside the doorway.

"I see that you don't understand. So come back out and go to the end of the line. We'll start again," I said in a very stern voice.

The students all hung their heads and began mumbling. I simply looked at them with a stony stare, and they quieted down. I sent the next five students in one at a time. The procedure continued until the students complied. We didn't have much class time left, but we were able to complete and discuss the drill. I collected the homework assignment from the previous day, and we discussed it. Then I explained the homework assignment for the day, and they copied the directions. I also included some of the class activities that we had not had the opportunity to complete as additional homework.

One of the teachers on my hall didn't like my tactics and went to my department head, Mr. Prose, to complain about what she termed "my mean treatment" toward the students and my elementary school tactics. Two days later, Mr. Prose came up my hall at the beginning of a period when I was scheduled to have a ninth-grade class. He found my students in a single file lined along the wall of my classroom. I was wearing a stern expression, walking up and down the line of students quietly demanding order.

I stood at the front of the line, Mr. Prose slowly walked over to me.

"Mrs. Artson, is everything all right?"

"Yes," I said. "I'm teaching my class the proper way to enter and behave in my classroom."

"Very good; keep it up." He said with a knowing smile.

With that, he left the hall. Later he sent me a note to see him in his office after school. I thought, *Oh God, now what?*

Mr. Prose was sitting at the work table in his office when I arrived. He smiled. I was shocked. *A smile twice in the same day*, I thought. He took his time before speaking to me, but when he began to speak, I knew I had won his admiration and respect. He spoke slowly in a very pleasant tone.

"Mrs. Artson, or should I call you Drill Sergeant?"

"Shirley is fine," I said with a pleasant smile.

"I like what I saw, letting students know that you're in charge."

"Thank you."

He pointed to a stack of books on the table. "There are the materials you requested. You may use the cart as long as you remember to return it tomorrow. Let me know if you need anything else. I've asked Ms. Dodd to be you mentor. She's in room 235. Feel free to ask her for assistance."

I thanked Mr. Prose, loaded the cart with the materials, and exited the office. I felt relieved and wonderfully accepted. I'd won him over without even trying. I was glad that I had not entered into a war with him.

After a couple weeks of repeatedly practicing how to enter and exit my classroom, the students finally got it. I discovered that ninth graders were like babies compared to students in the upper grades. They looked awkward and seemed out of place. They had not been adequately prepared at the middle school level for what to expect in high school. The students had been given a tour of the building, but they got lost often and were sometimes late to class for that reason. I decided to ask the guidance counselor to plan another tour of the building for them. She gladly agreed. I enjoyed working with my ninth graders. Despite their awkwardness and immaturity, I bonded with them very quickly. I was very strict with them, but they knew that I liked them, and they liked me too.

I think this was possible because I had experience working with that age group. The students were primarily from homes where emphasis was placed on educational expectations and students were encouraged to do well in school. I had excellent rapport with my students partly because I'd learned how to use incentives, praise, and rewards successfully. The students loved seeing their names on the Artson's Heroes bulletin board. I held their feet to the fire, but I gladly and quickly rewarded their efforts and success. I had an excellent relationship with my seniors too. I considered them young adults and treated them as such.

Lesson Learned

Encouraging students with rewards rather than penalties and punishment is an excellent strategy.

My seniors did not have a strong background in literature or writing. Needless to say, getting them through the twelfth-grade curriculum was no easy task. Twelfth-grade literature was British literature. It covered many of the works by Shakespeare, Browning, Chaucer, and other British writers. Students were expected to analyze the works using literary devices, to discuss the works, and to explore particular aspects of the various selections in writing.

One day I asked Melvin, a student in one of my senior classes, why he thought the author we were reading chose a particular dark setting for his story. "I don't know, Mrs. Artson. Maybe he was drunk, or maybe he just liked the dark. I do not know."

I asked him to look at the passage again to see if he could glean the reason.

"I told you the man was probably drunk, or maybe he didn't know it was dark. Frankly, Mrs. A, I don't care."

"The last comment was unnecessary, Melvin." I said.

Another student raised her hand.

"Are you also having problems with the assignment?" I asked.

"Mrs. Artson," she said solemnly. "I don't mean to be disrespectful, but this crap is too hard."

"I know it's difficult. Let's get through today, and I'll make some changes by tomorrow, okay."

These were the types of responses I received from my seniors regarding literature.

I spoke with Mr. Prose about the problems my students were having with the materials. His only comment was that the materials were required. Nonetheless, I knew that they were really struggling with the literature, so I found and purchased a set of low-readability, reproducible books that offered compilations of brief selections and emphasized the key points in the British literature selections in the text.

First, I taught the literary terms that were applicable to the selection, as well as the historical background of the selection. Then the students read the simplified version of the selection. When I was sure they had a clear understanding the work, I read aloud from the assigned text while they read silently. It worked! The students understood the literature and no longer disliked it as much. They could make sense of the selections, could discuss the selections, and could use the literary devices in their writing about them.

My seniors were not good writers, but they improved gradually. However, they struggled with the more formal writing assignments. Getting them through the research paper was like pulling teeth without Novocain. Again, I found low-level, simplified materials and taught the necessary skills at a slow pace. They were able to grasp it! I was really pleased with them and with myself. This was my first experience teaching British literature and the formal research paper. We made a good team. They knew they needed the skills in order to graduate, and I knew I needed to learn how to teach the skills. Together we survived. I knew that my kids needed something other than the required texts, and I was very glad to spend my own money on ancillary materials for my classes. These resources helped the students to master the skills, which in turn made it possible for me to accomplish the goals of the curriculum.

The students were happy as they learned; I was overjoyed as I taught. We were great together. Of course, on occasion a student had to be disciplined. On these occasions, I was careful to make sure that the disciplinary action was appropriate to the offense. I was becoming a good high school teacher. The wide gap in ages and maturity between the two groups I taught was a bit challenging, but I was getting very good at it. One of things that helped me was that my own children fell into both age groups.

Fortunately, I had a handle on the curriculum. It was really not difficult to follow, and I continued using ancillary materials. However, the Maryland Functional Tests were scheduled to be administered soon. Those tests were important, and I needed to know more about them in order to prepare my students appropriately. I decided to ask my mentor for help. Her classroom was directly across the hall from mine, and we were free during the same planning period. So I went to her room to ask for help with the tests.

Ms. Dodds sat at her desk reading what looked like students' papers. I knocked softly on her open door to get her attention. "Excuse me, Ms. Dodds, I was wondering if you'd share some information with me about the state tests." She shot me a glance that said, *Please leave me alone.*

"You need to see Mr. Prose about that," she said in a condescending tone.

"Mr. Prose said that you're my mentor and that I should see you for concerns."

She turned to face me with a hoity-toity expression. "Well, he certainly didn't tell me," she replied.

"I'm sorry to have bothered you," I said and left the room, annoyed and embarrassed. I vowed never to ask for her help again.

The following morning Ms. Dodds came to my room and offered to help me. She still had a haughty attitude but for some reason had decided to offer assistance. I too had an attitude—I was annoyed and didn't want to be bothered. I declined her offer. Fortunately, I was not without help. One of the other English teachers gave me copies of old ninth- and twelfth-grade reading and writing tests. I noticed right away that the reading test would not be a problem for my students because it was very basic. However, they needed a lot of help with the writing test.

I studied the old tests and the scoring criteria. The writing tests were in the form of prompts, which were basically situations for which students had to write resolutions. I decided to develop strategies and a format that would ensure that students understood the writing prompts. I taught my students to dissect and analyze the writing tasks for the purpose, structure, and details that needed to be included in their responses. I also taught them to plan each response by using a simple format that would ensure their responses were clear and written in correct language.

In addition, I emphasized to every class the importance of passing the state tests, and I offered incentives for attendance on test days and for a passing or near passing score. Most of all, the day prior to the test, I stressed that students do their very best. I had a very serious talk with each class.

"Do your best. That's all I ask of you. Please don't get nervous. I know you're prepared, just do your best. I need all students present on test days. Remember, if you pass the test this year, you will never have to take it again. However, if you do not pass it, you'll have to take it again next year. Eat a good breakfast tomorrow. I'll have donuts and juice here if you'd like stop by before school or during the day. Good luck to all of you."

Finally, it was time for the tests to be administered. I felt sure that they'd do a good job. I was correct; the pass rate for my students that year was great! I felt very proud of their success, as well as of my own. I was particularly proud because the tests were quite a big deal, and I'd taught myself how to prepare my students with strategies needed to pass the tests. I was more than happy to give my students the incentives they'd earned.

I continued to persevere in spite of the challenges I faced. I had the will, the strength, and the courage to do what was required to reach my goals and those of the system. I believe that being new at a task is not an acceptable excuse for failure. Because of my belief, the students and I worked hard, which resulted in a win-win situation.

"Every man must educate himself; his books and teacher are but help; the work is his."

Daniel Webster

Nine

Everything was moving in the right direction. The students and I were getting to know each better each day. Trust was established, and all seemed right with the world. I was grateful for the quick bond with my students. They were following the class rules and meeting curricular expectations. I couldn't have asked for more. Then one morning, Thomas, a ninth grader in my afternoon class, came rushing into my room. He was very excited. He paced the floor for a moment. I could tell that he had something on his mind. He finally spoke.

"Mrs. Artson, can I tell you something?" he asked.

"Thomas, you know that you can tell me anything."

"I mean, can I tell you something and you won't tell nobody?"

"I can't promise. It depends on what you're about to tell me. Don't you trust me?" I said, looking deeply and gently into his big brown eyes.

He paced a bit more; walking back and forth across the front of the room.

"I trust you, but this is serious."

"I can handle serious. Tell me."

"Okay. Mrs. Artson, Alan brought a jar of liquid cleaning stuff to school today. He put it in his locker. Said he is going to drink it."

"Why?" I inquired.

"I don't know, but please don't tell."

"Thomas, you're going to have to trust me. I promise that I'll handle this. I won't mention your name, and I won't do anything that might hurt Alan. Trust me. It'll be all right."

I gently placed my hands on his shoulders, reminded him that he could trust me, and told him to go to class.

I was not scheduled to see Alan until the afternoon. So I went to the guidance office, spoke briefly with his counselor in confidence, and got a copy of Alan's schedule. Then I went to his class and asked the teacher if I could speak with him. Alan smiled shyly when he noticed me. The teacher allowed him to leave with me. We chatted as we walked toward my room. When we entered the room, I smiled and asked him to be seated. He was becoming a little uneasy, so I pulled a chair up close, facing him and smiling all the while.

"Alan," I said softly. "Do you trust me?"

"Yes."

"I hear that you're upset about something. Is there anything I can do to help?"

He became anxious. A puzzled and fearful expression grew on his face, and he hung his head. "Alan, let's talk. What's bothering you?"

He began to cry, huge tears spilling down his cheeks. I handed him a box of tissues. Alan told me that his father beat him almost every day for one reason or another. He said that he was afraid of what his father might do to him if he knew that he was talking to me. He pulled up his shirt to show me old and new marks that covered his chest and abdomen. Then he turned his back to me and raised his shirt, revealing the very deep slashes on his back, some still bloody. He pulled up the legs of his pants to show similar bruises and welts on his legs. He said his backside looked like the rest of his body. The marks reminded me of pictures I'd seen of the bodies of slaves after they'd been brutally beaten. I could feel my eyes well with tears, which I fought to hold back. I asked the reason for the last beating.

"I would not take gym because I didn't want the kids to see the welts. Mr. Jones kept me after school and called my father."

"I'm so sorry, Alan. Don't worry. Everything is going to be all right."

"Please don't call my father, please," he pleaded.

"I promise you, I will not do that. You have my word."

"What are you going to do?"

"Alan, I have to report what happened. By law, I must. I'll get in big trouble with the law if I do not. But please know this, I will not allow anything to happen to you. You're going to have to trust me. Can you do that?"

"Will I have to go home?"

"No. You are going to be placed in child protective custody." I explained what that meant, and he seemed relieved. However, I wanted the jar of bleach.

"Alan, do you have a jar of some type of household cleaner in your locker?"

"Yes."

"What did you plan to do with it?"

"Drink it so I could die."

"Alan, if you did that it would break my heart."

By this time, my eyes had filled with tears, and they spilled down my cheeks.

"Please don't do that, Alan. Give me the jar."

"Don't cry. I'll give it to you. We have to go to my locker to get it. Please don't cry, Mrs. Artson."

I regained my composure, and we walked slowly to his locker. He opened the locker, reached in, and pulled out a quart jar half filled with lemon household cleaner. I could smell it before he handed it to me. For a moment, I just held the jar in my hand and looked at Alan sadly. It scared me to death to think that this child was actually going to drink household cleaner and that he was so frightened he'd decided to choose death rather than continue to live in the hell in which he obviously did. I couldn't help myself. I reached out, pulled him to me, and hugged him for a long moment. I did not consider what the people passing in the hall would think. I just needed to comfort Alan. He lifted his head and smiled at me, a shy, grateful smile. I knew that I had to complete a child abuse report, and I was not looking forward to it. However, I knew that it was best for Alan.

"Alan," I said. "Will you do one more thing for me?"

"What?"

"Will you go with me to the guidance office and talk with Mrs. Richmond?"

He hesitated briefly.

"Trust me, Alan. It'll be all right. Nothing bad will happen to you."

"Okay, Mrs. Artson, I'll go. Will I see you again today?"

"Yes. I won't leave school until I find out how things are with you."

When we reached the office, I directed Alan to a chair while I went to find Mrs. Richmond. I explained the situation to her in detail and gave her the jar. I told her that Alan was in a very delicate state, extremely afraid to go home, and that I was leaving him in her care. She promised that she would do her very best for him. I returned to where he was sitting with Mrs. Richmond. She gave Alan a warm, friendly smile that made him feel at ease, and he returned the smile. I told Alan that I would see him later. I stopped by to see Alan before I left school. He was comfortable with Mrs. Richmond. So I just smiled, and he said, "See you later."

Alan was not in school for a few days. He'd been placed in protective custody. Wednesday of the following week, I heard his happy voice in the hall, and I couldn't contain my joy. I rushed into the hall. He saw me and gave me a broad grin and thumbs up. I grinned too and went back in my classroom. Many years later, I saw Alan. He gave me a hug and said that he often thinks of me and remembers me fondly.

Lesson Learned

Trust between student and teacher is valuable; it benefits both.

Greener Grasses High was a good school. However, I rarely saw the principal. I occasionally passed him in the hall and was never sure if he knew who I was. To most people at the school, I was the lady from the School of Hard Knocks. I think that most people predicted that I would not make it there. Unfortunately, most high teachers looked down their noses at junior high school teachers. After a couple of years at Greener Grasses High School, the administrators and teachers accepted me as a member of the crew.

Like junior high school, one of the greatest pains in the posterior that high school teachers have to endure is the ever-daunting instructional observation. I was observed by Mr. Prose during the first quarter of the school year. He sat straight-faced in the back of my classroom, watching my every move, listening critically to every word that came out my mouth and out of students' mouths, writing his judgments of my performance. At the end of the period, he left the room without a smile or a nod.

Prior to the observation, the class had been working on writing and delivering three-minute speeches. I did not want to change the skill in midstream. I decided to continue with speeches as planned. The students were doing a very good job of providing positive feedback for the speakers.

On the day of the observation, I'd scheduled ten students to deliver their speeches. The class and I would act as both the audience and evaluators. Students were given score sheets that required them to not only score the delivery of the speeches but also to make helpful comments. I would collect the sheets and add my comments. The score sheets were then returned to the students. After all the speeches were delivered, we would discuss the strengths and weaknesses in each speech.

Mr. Prose was not pleased with the presentations. He criticized me for not interrupting the students while they were speaking to correct their usage errors. I explained that the purpose of the activity was to help make students more comfortable with oral discussion and to encourage them to verbally express their ideas. I also explained the score sheets. He insisted that I should have corrected the students' errors in grammar while they were delivering the speeches.

Although I explained that I did not want to discourage the students' efforts or embarrass them, he seemed rigid in his decision. However, I stood up to him, held my ground, and insisted that he give the lesson a fair rating. I refused to accept his rating. He didn't like the fact that I stood up to him, but he did change the rating. Later, he told me that I was very feisty. He respected my courage to make a stand for what I believed.

I was observed later in the year by one of the English specialists from the central office. She sat in the back of the room and wrote the entire time, rarely looking up from the paper. Her rating of the lesson was not favorable. She claimed that I said "Okay now" twenty times during the lesson, and she didn't like it. Once more, I had to assert myself. It was quite a battle, but I won. My assertiveness caused her to respect me, and she never did that again. Later, we became close associates.

It was necessary for me to fight for respect from most of my superiors by using strength, talent, and intelligence. I advise new teachers to refuse to be bullied and to be less concerned about being liked. It is much more important to be respected.

Lesson Learned

You can be victorious in battle if you have the courage to remain firm in your own convictions.

The next few months were uneventful. The seniors worked hard to complete a major curriculum requirement for graduation: the formal research paper. They struggled; writing was a class weakness. I offered to work with them before school, during my planning and lunch periods, and after school. Most of them had jobs or other responsibilities and could not remain after school. Therefore, they elected to work during the other posted times. This was actually better for me too, because it was difficult for me to stay after school for any length of time.

Another problem for the seniors was the work-study program. This was a vocational-technical high school, and in various technical skill areas work-study was part of the training. These were salaried jobs in the students' career paths. Many of the seniors had work-study jobs and were often absent from class. Students in the program were responsible for keeping up with their academic studies. However, several fell behind and needed assistance.

The work-study program was a privilege, not a right. Students who fell behind in their studies or who exhibited behavioral problems were dropped from the program. For this reason, Alex was having great difficulty. He had missed several assignments and was behind on the research project. Alex was a nice young man and one of our best football players. He was over six feet tall and weighed approximately one hundred and seventy pounds. He'd received deficiency notices for senior English and other classes. One day he stayed after class to talk with me about his problem.

"Mrs. Artson, I'm not doing very good in your class, am I?"

"Let's see." I said reaching for my grade-book. We sat side by side. I covered the other students' grades, and we looked at his grades.

"Alex, you are missing several grades. If you would get those in it would help."

"Okay, but I'm really having trouble with the research paper."

"I'll help you, but you'll have to make yourself available."

"I work after school."

"You may come before school or during your lunch period. We have the same lunch period."

He screwed his mouth around in an indecisive manner, stretched, and sighed.

"It's your call. I'll help, but you have to be willing to work with me."

"I'll be here. Just say when."

We arranged a schedule for the tutoring sessions. I gave him a number of make-up assignments, and we worked together on the research paper. I'd created a written strategy called *Stepping Down the Research Paper* and had given it to all my seniors. It consisted of twelve objectives, beginning with selecting and narrowing the topic and ending with the completed final copy of the paper. I taught each step prior to having the students practice it and apply it to their papers. Alex had not looked at the sheet once. He was really behind. It was nearly time for students to hand in their first drafts, and he hadn't done any of it.

"Alex, when I give a handout, you're expected to read it and use it."

"I know Mrs. Artson. I messed up. I'm sorry.

"Apology accepted. Now let's get to work."

I guided him through all the objectives for completing the research paper. He came to all the scheduled tutoring sessions and always completed his assigned tasks. He was late finishing his research project, but he produced a good paper.

I really wanted my seniors to graduate. They were good students and worked hard to meet expectations. Fortunately, all of my seniors passed. They were excited as was I.

One day while I was on hall duty outside my room, Alex rushed up to me, scooped me up in his arms, swung me around, and planted a big kiss on my cheek. It happened so quickly, I could do nothing except tell him quietly and firmly to put me down. He complied but held me at arm's length. He grinned the most wonderful smile, broad and genuine.

"Thank you for helping me, Mrs. Artson, and for talking to my other teachers. I'm graduating. I'll never forget you."

He left me standing there, the other teachers on the hall glaring at me with expressions of disapproval and puzzlement.

The senior farewell was the next day. During the assembly, the students willed certain things to the school and to teachers, all in fun. The senior class that year left me a twenty-page research paper.

"And to Mrs. Artson we bequeath a twenty-page ding-dang research paper."

Lesson Learned

To be effective, teacher intelligence is crucial, but caring is more critical.

I remained at Greener Grasses High School three more years. During my last year there, I prepared for a new challenge. I wanted to be promoted to English department head, which would mean that I would train and supervise other English teachers. I'd completed my graduate work and received a Master of Science in School Administration and Supervision, but I still needed to take a national exam. I also had to be interviewed by a panel of administrators. Both were requirements for the promotion. I took the administration and supervision exam and received the required score for the promotion. It was not an easy exam, so I gave myself thumbs up for passing it. I was now eligible for the interview. Although I had no idea what types of questions would be asked, I felt ready to face the panel of interviewers.

There was really no way to prepare for the interview. There was no way of knowing what types of questions would be asked. I'd heard from others who'd taken the interview that it was grueling. However, I was not discouraged. I had survived the School of Hard Knocks and Greener Grasses High School and passed the national exam, and I'd survive the interview too.

The day of the interview, I dressed in my lucky navy blue suit and a soft white blouse. When I arrived at the site, I was ushered into a waiting area where five obviously very nervous people sat to wait for their times to be interviewed. Watching them was making me nervous too.

I left the area for a few moments, stood in the hall, and fixed my mind on other things. When it was my turn to be interviewed, I calmly walked into the conference room and waited to be directed to sit. I sat at one end of a very long table, opposite the lead interviewer. Nine very poker-faced administrators sat around the table. They never smiled. Each of the administrators asked a question. The questions were only stated once. Some questions were two-part, and both parts had to be answered.

Fortunately, I was able to answer all the questions completely, some better than others. After I answered the last question, the lead interviewer simply dismissed me without a smile. "Thank you for coming," she said. That ended the interview.

As I left, I thought, *Gee, they should call this an interrogation.* It did not feel like an interview; it felt more like a cross-examination. Two weeks later, I received a letter in the mail informing me that I'd passed the interview and that my name was now listed in the pool among the top five eligible department heads. The only thing left to do was to wait to be selected by a school principal. I was absolutely thrilled beyond expression.

One day near the end of the first semester, I received a call from the main office informing me that there was a vacancy for an English department head at Mountain View High School. I was directed to call the principal to arrange an interview. Needless to say, I was ecstatic. I felt featherlight as I practically floated down the hall to my classroom. In the quiet of my room, I sat and reflected on my professional journey. I could barely contain my excitement, and there was no one at school with whom to share my good news. I was anxious to go home, tell my children, and call my family and friends.

The next morning I called Mountain View High School. I was told that the secretary would call me back with an appointment. Two days later, I received a call from the principal, Dr. Freeman. We discussed the best time for the interview and decided to have it at 2:00 PM, the next day. I informed Mr. Prose immediately, because I needed coverage for my afternoon classes. He was not at all excited for me. He glided around the office and in a pooh-pooh manner said, "Well, I didn't know you were interested in being a department head. Go ahead; I'll get coverage for your classes." I smiled and thanked him. After school, I rushed home to check my wardrobe. I decided to wear a black skirt and white blouse.

I arrived at work the following day at my usual time and followed my usual routines. Inside I wanted to scream with joy. I wore a noticeable smile on my face. I wasn't worried about the interview. I'd recently completed the interview from hell, and I believed that if I could get through that and come out on top, this one would be a piece of cake. My excitement was apparent to my students, and they commented. One said, "Mrs. Artson, you seem really happy today. What's up?"

"I'm just happy. I'll tell you later if things work out for me."

The morning seemed to drag by. I waited for 1:00 PM so I could leave for my appointment. When it was finally time for me to leave, I collected my things, signed out, and left the building. I was a few minutes early for my appointment and was greeted by a very friendly office staff. The secretary invited me to have a seat and informed Dr. Freeman that I was sitting in the waiting area.

He came out of his office, greeted me with a pleasant smile and warm hand shake, and escorted me into his office. He seemed like a genuinely nice person. We connected immediately. He told me that the current department head was transferring to another school. Dr. Freeman talked about the department's strengths and weaknesses. He said he needed someone who could take charge, run the department without coming to him for every little thing, and whip it in shape. He was not happy about the state test scores and other problems in the department.

"I'd like to hire you, Mrs. Artson, if you're interested."

"Yes, I'm interested," I beamed.

"Department heads here also teach," he said.

"I'm still interested."

"You will teach journalism; we have a newspaper. You'll teach English IV, and you will be responsible for publishing our annual magazine."

"How often is the newspaper published?"

"I'll leave that up to you."

"When would I start?"

"Mrs. Holster is leaving in two weeks. I'd like you in place by that time, and I'd like you to come here a few times before she leaves so that she can show you around and transfer the department to you. I'd like a smooth transition."

"I am happy to accept the position," I said happily.

Dr. Freeman shook my hand, welcomed me, and said that he would call my principal and make all the arrangements.

Although Dr. Freeman said that he'd contact my principal, I knew that I should also speak with him and let him know that I would be leaving to accept a promotion. Dr. Stanfield was relatively new to our school. He'd only been principal there two years. He was a quiet, reserved man who spent most of his time in his office. He was rarely seen in the halls and never on my floor. I don't believe he ever left the first floor. The students didn't know him, and he surely did not know them. He barely knew the teachers.

I decided to see him during my lunch period. I tapped lightly on his open door. He looked up from the paperwork on his desk. He didn't smile or frown. He had a blank and confused expression on his face.

"Yes," he said slowly.

"Dr. Stanfield, I'm Mrs. Artson. Dr. Freeman said that he would contact you about my promotion."

"Who?"

"Dr. Freeman, the principal at Mountain View High School"

"Oh, yes, you're Mrs. Artson." It was more a question than a statement.

"Yes."

"You have my permission to go to Mountain View a few half days to work with the department head. Please rotate mornings and afternoons so that you won't miss the same classes."

"That's fine. Thank you."

"Congratulations on your promotion. Dr. Freeman and I will handle everything."

He reached across his desk and shook my hand loosely. I smiled and left his office.

I was thrilled about my promotion but not happy about leaving my students. I had a full ninth-grade schedule that year, and I was concerned that they would feel abandoned. I was reluctant to tell them but knew I must. I told all of my classes on the same day. They were disappointed and a little sad but wished me well.

I spent four half days with Mrs. Holster, the current department head. She told me about all the teachers in the department. They obviously liked her; however, she did not speak favorably about them. There were eighteen teachers in the English department. Four were special educators. Several had been teaching there since the school had opened more than twenty years prior. The teachers did not want Mrs. Holster to leave. She, on the other hand, was jumping for joy. When I inquired about her jubilance she said, "You'll understand soon enough." She then told me about the teachers' bad habits but refused to identify which teachers owned which habits.

"One teacher is late every morning, and her colleague covers for her. One is late returning from lunch at least three times a week. One is very brazen and arrogant. You'll recognize her right away. What's more, they all dance to the beat of their own drums. I wish you good luck," Mrs. Holster said in a matter-of-fact manner and walked away.

She told me so many negative things about the teachers that for a brief moment I thought, *Now what have you gotten yourself into, Shirley?* but I quickly dismissed the feeling of impending doom. Dr. Freeman expected me to pull the department together and to get it on the right track and that I would surely do. I observed the teachers informally from a distance for the two weeks I spent with Mrs. Holster. I observed their attendance, including lateness to school, and their returning times from lunch. I noticed which teachers covered for each other. I also observed the classroom environments.

I made it a point to greet each teacher every day during the transition. Their manners were very cold and unwelcoming. I realized immediately that it would be difficult for me to get to know them. They wanted nothing to do with me. In fact, they seemed to resent me. There was only one teacher who readily accepted me, a special education teacher. She did her best to make me feel welcome and comfortable. She became my ally. I was not concerned about the others because cold, unfriendly personalities in the workplace were not new to me. I'd encountered them at both previous schools. The fact was I had a job to do, and I was going to do it. However, I did want a good working relationship with the teachers who I was assigned to supervise.

"What then is education? Surely, gymnastics for the body and music for the mind."

Plato

Ten

Once I was officially in the position and the time was right, I scheduled a department meeting. My main objective was to establish a few much-needed expectations. I introduced myself and explained my goals. Most of the teachers exhibited antagonistic, pompous attitudes. Mrs. Oliver, my ally, smiled and remained pleasant. An attempt was made by some of the teachers, led by Ms. Lucy Buzibod, to disrupt the meeting by tuning out what I was saying and having conversations of their own. I simply said, "I've shown you all respect, and I'd appreciate it if you'd do the same for me."

The teachers became quiet, but facial expressions let me know that they resented the comment. I continued the meeting, emphasizing the necessity for developing unit plans and for writing a detailed daily lesson plan. I also made reference to the things that I'd observed. I commented on both the positive and the negative, including concerns about attendance and lateness. I asked teachers to contact me if they were going to be late or absent. They made a fuss about everything I said. The teachers were not accustomed to being held to these standards, and they did not like the new rules at all. I ended the meeting by asking each of them to schedule an appointment with me sometime during the following week for individual conferences. They grumbled and complained as they exited. When the teachers had all left the room, I sat and thought about my meeting with Dr. Freeman and fully understood his concerns.

The situation was not easy for me, but I could not waste my time worrying about the teachers' attitudes or whether they liked me. I knew that I would eventually gain their respect, and that was all that truly mattered. However, it soon became apparent that the teachers wanted me out. They attempted to file a grievance against me with the teachers' union. They were told by the union representative that they could not grieve my personality or leadership style. I had not infringed on any of their rights, and there was nothing to grieve. That didn't satisfy them. So most of them got together and practically stormed the principal's office to complain about me. Dr. Freeman told them that I was doing my job. He reprimanded them for their tactics. The problem was the teachers had been allowed to do whatever they liked and were stubborn die-hards who suffered from the Frank Sinatra Syndrome: They wanted to *do it their way.*

One benefit of my new position was that I was now in the same school as my friend Trudy from the School of Hard Knocks. We resumed having lunch together, and I enjoyed the comfort of her friendship. And even though most of the teachers in my department were resistant, the students were not. They were typical urban high school teens. I didn't need to be concerned about student discipline because department heads were pseudo-administrators, with the authority to suspend. I did experience a minor instructional problem; I had to learn how to teach journalism so that I could teach the class. I learned quickly, and we published two issues that semester. I was also able to get merchants in the community to sponsor the paper. It was great.

I was exhausted by the end of the year but gained some ground with many of the teachers in my department. Furthermore, although I was new to the school, I belonged to an exclusive group. As a department head, I was not isolated as I had been as a classroom teacher. I could go to any of the department heads for assistance. And at the end of school year, a couple of the teachers transferred to other schools. This meant that the following year I'd have a few new teachers in my department. I had a heart for new teachers because of all that I'd been through, and I intended to do everything in my power to give them a good start. The school year closed on a positive note, and I looked forward to the next year.

Lesson Learned

Self-restraint, tolerance, and conviction triumph over difficulty.

My heart's desire was to become an advocate for new teachers and transfer teachers from other schools. I loved training and supporting them, and I understood their frustrations, fears, and insecurities. Teaching can be so overwhelming, especially for first-year teachers. Many of the tasks are tremendous; including developing unit plans, writing the daily lesson plan, selecting the appropriate materials, grading papers, recording grades, contacting parents, and attending meetings, to name only a few. Just thinking about the demands of the job makes me tired.

Another area of frustration for new teachers is the number and levels of supervisors. It seems that everybody tells the new teacher what to do. Unfortunately, not everyone directs the teacher to do the task in the same manner. This can cause even more frustration. However, this is something that new teachers must learn to handle successfully.

So I became a mentor for new teachers. I could honestly relate to them. I did not want any of my new teachers to feel as isolated and lost as I'd felt. I made them a priority in my day. Most were bright and knowledgeable in the subject area. However, many had difficulty with the numerous departmental tasks and the rigorous curricular structure that teachers must follow, as well as with the school and system rules and procedures new teachers must learn and adopt.

And there is the day-to-day struggle of working with unruly students who curse like sailors, call the teacher profane names, and refuse to do the work in class or to complete home assignments, as well as the students who create daily pandemonium in the classroom. New teachers are often reluctant to refer students to the office because they don't want to be considered weak. The occasional times they do make referrals, feedback is rarely provided. The teacher never knows what actions were taken by the administration.

I've had new teachers come to me in tears, quit midsemester, or give up and allow their job performance to suffer. One of my new teachers quit the profession to become a veterinarian. She wrote me a nice letter thanking me for helping her but said that she "just couldn't take it anymore." New teachers often have difficulty connecting with students without forming a buddy-buddy relationship. New teachers don't always know where to draw the line and often feel they need the students' friendship to get and maintain order in the class. I have allowed new teachers to literally cry on my shoulder. Above all, I've been blessed to be able to establish long-lasting relationships with several of my new teachers.

Dr. Freeman was very good to me. He stood with me when the teachers tried to attack me. He gave me full authority to run my department and supported all of the decisions I made. But principals are rarely supportive toward new teachers. When it came to recognizing and supporting the new teachers, he fell short as an advocate and was no different from other principals for whom I'd worked.

I understood the plight of new teachers and was more than happy to assist them. I shared the experiences of my first year with them. I wanted to assure them that what they were going through was not unique. I also tried to support the veteran teachers as well. They, on the other hand, did not want any advice or help from me. It was difficult for them to change their methods.

I really liked my new position as a department head; it allowed me to both supervise and to teach. It was a good place to be. The teachers also liked the fact that I taught classes because it put me somewhat on their level, not above them. I did not present myself as being superior to them. We taught the same type of students with the same issues and behaviors.

Some of the students at Mountain View High School were respectful to adults, and others were not. Some really gave teachers a hard time. I did not have classroom management problems because I'd learned how to manage student behavior, but I sympathized with the new teachers who had not reached that level of management.

Lesson Learned

With courage, persistence, and unshrinking patience, one can accomplish the impossible.

The following year at Mountain View High School, I had three new teachers in my department. One was a transfer teacher from another school, and the other two were from the Teach for America program. The transfer teacher, Ms. Felicia Stivin, was a capable special education teacher who didn't need much help. The other two, Miss Daisie Shore and Miss Susie Bethany, were new teachers who needed a great deal of help. I discovered this during my first meeting with them, so I took them under my wing right away.

They had not had a tour of the building, so I did that first. I pointed out the places that they would frequent: the rest room on each floor, the library, cafeteria, guidance office, auditorium, sign-in and mailbox areas in the main office, English book room, my office, and their classrooms. Then I sat with them for a long time, went over relevant department information, and answered the many questions they had. I gave each of them a box of supplies, a copy of the curriculum, and the teacher's edition of all texts for their classes. They were then dismissed to work in their classrooms.

I made sure that I was available for the questions I knew they'd have later, and I scheduled a meeting with them to discuss instructional matters. I also scheduled weekly individual support meetings for the first few months of the school year. I knew there would be many questions and concerns once the new teachers started working with the curriculum.

Although I was a new department head, I had learned a great deal during the previous semester and was comfortable in my position. That particular year I'd been assigned the yearbook class. It had been another teacher's assignment for many years, and she was not at all happy about the fact that Dr. Freeman had taken it from her. However, he was not pleased with the manner in which she had handled it the past few years.

I did not want the assignment. I didn't know a ding-dang thing about how to produce a yearbook. I objected to the assignment, but Dr. Freeman simply and calmly said, "The yearbook is one of the classes in your department. You should know how to produce it. It falls under your supervision, like all the other classes." All my objections didn't change his mind. The class was mine whether I wanted it or not; I would have to learn how to teach the class and produce the yearbook. I had a conference with the teacher who'd previously taught the class. I informed her that I did not ask for the class, nor did I want it, but Dr. Freeman had insisted I teach the class. I asked for her assistance and for all the yearbook materials. She gave me very few materials and little information about the class.

Although Dr. Freeman assigned me the yearbook class, he discontinued the quarterly magazine that I'd produced and replaced it with responsibility for the senior graduation booklet. That year, in addition to supervising the department and producing the lengthy graduation booklet, I taught two classes: yearbook and African American literature. It was truly a learning experience

I was not sure what to do with the yearbook class. I didn't even know where to start. So I called a teacher at another school who taught yearbook. She met with me a few times until I was comfortable with teaching the class. The yearbook publishing representative was also very helpful, and the students were great. I included all of the students' ideas in the book; they did all the work. I supervised it and proofread their copy. It turned out to be a nice class. All the students in the class were seniors, and it was their book, which motivated them to do a good job. I ran the class informally. Students were divided in groups by book sections. They were allowed to talk and be sociable as long as they did the work. The class produced a very good book, except for one glaring spelling error.

I caught the mistake when the books were delivered to the school. The publisher was willing to correct it and reprint the books because the error was actually not mine; it was the publisher's. However, Dr. Freeman was determined that the books would be distributed to students on time. Therefore, he refused to allow me to correct the error, and it was released with the glaring spelling mistake. Although I placed an editor's apology at the front of the book, I was very embarrassed about the error. Needless to say, the teacher who previously taught the class happily gloated about my situation. She couldn't point it out to enough people.

I learned from the mistake and taught the class for three years. Later, a new principal was assigned to the school. He agreed that I should not teach the class and reassigned it to the former yearbook teacher. I was happy and she was ecstatic.

Except for the yearbook class, I was delighted with the way that things were going that year. The teachers were finally working together as a unit. There were still the die-hards, but even they were improving their stinkpot attitudes. The new teachers, Miss Shore and Miss Bethany, were attending the individual support meetings. Ms. Stivin came to see me on an as-needed basis.

But within a few weeks, I noticed that Miss Shore and Miss Bethany were not attending their individual support meetings. I observed them from a distance for a week and noticed problems. I decided to make brief visits to their rooms and noticed that both teachers were having problems. I did not understand why they'd stop coming for help when it was very obvious that they still needed assistance. I thought about the situation for a while. Finally, I decided to approach them. One day while they were standing in the hall talking, I took the opportunity to talk with them.

"Hi. How are you both?"

"Fine," they said in unison.

"Why did you guys stop coming to the support meetings?"

"Ms. Buzibod said that we don't have to give up our planning periods to meet with you if we don't want to," Miss Bethany confessed.

"Oh," I said. "Is Miss Buzibod now your department head?"

"No, but we can use the time for other things," Miss Shore admitted.

"Were the meetings helping either of you?"

"Yes," they agreed in unison.

"I don't recall ever saying that the meetings were mandatory. They were scheduled to help you, but if you feel that you don't need or want the help, you do not have to attend the meetings. However, you should know that in addition to helping you do a better job, I was preparing you for the upcoming informal classroom observation," I said with a smile.

They looked at each other for the appropriate response.

Again in unison, they said, "I'd rather do other things."

I wished them a pleasant day and slowly walked away. I was a little disappointed that my help was rejected. I knew that they would regret it later, but I could not force the help on them. Every new teacher needs help in the beginning, and most desire it. However, this pair felt that they did not need help and certainly did not want it. I thought, *When I first started this journey I would have given my eye teeth to have my supervisor offer the help that I am offering to them.* I licked my wounds and moved on.

I allowed a few days to pass before approaching Ms. Buzibod. I firmly believe that the best way to stop abuse of any kind is to expose or confront the abuser. One afternoon after the students had been dismissed, I went to her room to talk with her. She was seated at her desk.

"Hi, Ms. Buzibod. May I have a few minutes of your time?"

"Sure," she answered in a gruff tone.

"Miss Shore and Miss Bethany told me that you advised them not to continue the support meetings with me."

Her facial expression and body language revealed her irritation. She stood up and assumed a very hostile stance, arms folded under her bosom and head tilted to one side.

"That is not what I said," she snarled.

"Nevertheless, you are interfering where you should not. These ladies really need help, and they were benefiting from the conferences. I am not here to argue with you. I am here to suggest that you not discourage them from getting the help they desperately need. Obviously, they like and trust you. If you really want to help them, don't dissuade them from accepting assistance. Thank you, and enjoy your evening."

I left her standing with her hands on her ample hips and exited the room.

When I conducted the informal instructional observations of Miss Shore and Miss Bethany later, I found several weaknesses. In each case, I entered the classroom on time, smiled, and took a seat in the back of the room. Neither teacher gave me a copy of the lesson plan, nor did they give me the other materials I'd requested. Also I found numerous weaknesses before, during, and after the lesson. Although both lesson plans were beautifully typed, both lacked the required components, and the classroom environment in each case was inappropriate.

Students laughed at improper times and held private conservations unrelated to the lesson. There was no sense of established class rules or order in their rooms. Although an objective was written on the chalkboards as required, in both cases it was stated incorrectly and resembled Ms. Buzibod's format. In both cases there were many problems that could have easily been corrected if they had asked for help. Nonetheless, it was my responsibility to meet with each teacher and indicate the strengths as well as the weaknesses in the lessons.

I completed the written reports of the lessons. I didn't want to squash their enthusiasm. Therefore, I decided not to discuss every weakness but to focus on the most outstanding ones. The conferences were almost identical. I met with Miss Shore first. She came in smiling and received a smile in return from me. I began by pointing out the strengths of her lesson. It is my belief that observers can always find something positive about a teacher's performance. Next, I mentioned the major weaknesses I observed in the lesson, as well as the missing instructional items. I also discussed the classroom climate with each teacher.

Miss Shore was quiet. She knew that I was being truthful and not nitpicky. She took the news well and asked if she could resume the support meetings. Miss Bethany's conference went much the same. In the end, they both decided to accept the help offered, and I was happy to assist them. In a way, I saw their success as my success. In fact, by the end of the first semester, both teachers had really blossomed. The teachers and I ended the weekly support meetings and decided that they would ask for help if they needed it. They became my champions and developed good relationships with me. Almost every year that I was at Mountain View High School, I had at least one new teacher. There was a great turnover of new teachers. Nationwide, approximately 30 percent of all new teachers leave the profession within the first five years. It seems that if they are able to tough it out for five years, most will stay much longer. I enjoyed working with new teachers and was a little sad to see most of my new teachers leave.

In addition to working with teachers, as a pseudo-administrator I not only disciplined students of teachers in my department but students in the halls and in other places where they were misbehaving. In so doing, I discovered that high school males are sometimes more difficult to handle than females. Also young men of that age are very frisky, and female teachers have to be careful how they interact with them.

When I was working at Mountain View High School, I was in my mid-forties, weighed one hundred and twenty pounds, and had curves in all the right places. I didn't dress provocatively, but it was impossible to hide my figure. One day I was walking in the hall; three young men were walking behind me, laughing and talking. They really should have been in class. They obviously noticed my derrière. One said to the others in an audible voice, "Yeah. I believe I like the junk in that trunk."

They all laughed and continued making comments about my behind. I stopped suddenly and turned around to face them. They were startled and stood there with deer-in-the-headlights expressions on their faces. I looked straight into their faces.

"What did you say?" I asked, calmly but firmly.

"Who? Me? Nothin'," the one in the middle said.

"Then which one of you made the comment?"

"What comment?" the one on the right asked.

"You know what comment. It was neither nice nor respectful. Where do you all belong? Get to class!" I ordered before they could answer. They took off at a trot. "Smelling your musk," I mumbled as I continued down the hall.

Lesson Learned

Understanding the foolishness of young men is beneficial to teachers.

Another time I passed a group of young men loitering in the hall.

"Where do you gentlemen belong?" I asked. "Get to class; you're late."

One of the young men looked at me with a hostile expression.

"Arrh, go piss up a pole!" he shouted.

I simply raise a brow, looked him directly in the face, and made a sweeping arm movement from my waist across my pelvis area, indicating anatomy 101. I asked, "How?"

His buddies got it immediately. One said, still laughing, "Oh man, she scored on you."

Then the others laughed and pointed their fingers at him. He was angry and embarrassed.

"Shut up!" he shrieked.

The group moved further down the hall, still teasing Mr. Smarty Pants. I chuckled to myself as I walked away.

I continued teaching and training teachers at Mountain View High School for a few more years. At that point, I felt that I was ready for a new challenge. I decided to try my hand at administration. With that in mind, I prepared to interview for the position of assistant principal. I talked to a few people who'd recently passed the interview and was given an idea of the types of questions I might be asked. The interview format was the same interrogative method as the one I'd experienced previously for department head.

I passed the interview, and my name was added to the list of eligible assistant principals. Later, I was interviewed for a position by Dr. E. Bellicose, principal of Broadside Middle School, one of the largest middle schools in west Baltimore. Dr. Bellicose was impressed with my background and interests and was anxious to hire me immediately. I accepted the offer and left Mountain View High School for a position as assistant principal at Broadside Middle School.

I was hired as the new eighth-grade house principal, in charge of all the students, faculty, and support staff in the eighth-grade wing of the school. I got off to a very good start. The sixth- and seventh-grade principals were very supportive, taught me most of what I needed to know, and were available to provide any help I needed. It was the first year that I had not taught since I began my career. It felt strange in the beginning, but I soon adjusted. It took time for the teachers and students to get used to my leadership. Both soon learned that I was friendly and supportive but no-nonsense.

I was very content in my position. At first, I liked Dr. Bellicose. He seemed quite genuine. However, the more I got to know him, the more concerned I became about my decision to come to his school. I noticed that he did many mean and hateful things to teachers, office staff, and support staff for no good reason. He did these cruel things simply because he could. He was spiteful and seemed to be always looking for a fight. He was also belligerent, antagonistic, and hostile. I came to understand him as a despicable man who thoroughly enjoyed hurting others. He was as ornery as a rattlesnake and just as deadly.

Meanwhile, he was attempting to train me to behave in the same manner. For example, he had a very strict policy on teachers signing in on time. In order to get them to come to work on time, he wanted the sign-in book removed from the counter at exactly 8:30 AM, even if a teacher was standing at the counter with pen in hand. He wanted to make this my charge, but I refused to do it. Dr. Bellicose also docked paychecks for a number of days if someone did something that he did not like or refused to do what he wanted; regardless whether it was his or her duty or not. There came a time when he docked my paycheck two days because I was ill and could not come to work. Docked days were always restored, but it took two or more pay periods for the money to be refunded. I began to understand why the faculty and staff referred to Dr. Bellicose as Dr. Lucifer. He had the personality and spirit of Lucifer and Adolf Hitler incarnate.

Finally, I decided that I could not continue to work under his leadership and requested a transfer to another school, which made Dr. Bellicose very angry. He blocked my transfer, and I filed a grievance. I did not realize when I was hired as assistant principal that there was a school board policy that stated that a newly assigned assistant principal must remain at the assigned school for two full school years before a transfer could be granted. I was confused because I had cleared my transfer request with the AEO, Dr. Luciferina Daemony. She said that she understood my reason for the transfer request and would support me. However, it was later revealed that she was not an honest person.

Dr. Bellicose was furious about the grievance I filed and tried to have me demoted back to classroom teacher. Dr. George Nobleman was the CEO of Baltimore City Public Schools at the time. He refused to demote me. He did, however; uphold the board's two-year policy. He gave me two choices: I could continue at Broadside Middle School for another year and transfer at that time, or I could return to department head status and keep my assistant principal salary for a year. I gladly chose the latter. Dr. Bellicose was very shocked and disappointed. He thought that I wanted to be an assistant principal so badly that I would choose to return to his school. He was very wrong. I have never regretted my decision.

Lesson Learned

Sometimes hard choices must be made. It's always best to choose on the side of right.

I was happy about the opportunity to return to department head status; it was more my forte. It was equally wonderful to retain my assistant principal salary for an entire year. It was just a matter of finding a vacancy for a high school English department head. While I was waiting for a position, a friend who was the principal of an elementary school asked me to fill in for her assistant principal, who was out on sick leave. I accepted and worked for her one semester before receiving a position as department head in a high school.

It was near the end of the semester when I discovered that there was a vacancy for an English department head at Promise High School in east Baltimore. I applied and was accepted. The principal, Mrs. Phyllis Fortress, was a retired administrator from one of the surrounding counties. Tough but fair, she was very strong on discipline and instruction. I worked as her special assistant for the remainder of the school year. She gave me a huge office and all the resources I needed. I worked very closely with teachers on instruction and conducted formal observations. The next year, Mrs. Fortress asked me to take the English department head position.

Mrs. Fortress gave me many opportunities to grow. We worked very closely together. She was the best principal I ever worked for. She understood the plight of teachers and made sure that all new teachers were treated with respect and given the resources and support they needed. Unfortunately, she left Promise High School after two years for a school in her community. I left Promise High at the end of the following year and took a position as assistant to the director of school closings and reorganization at school headquarters. I was injured while working there and decided, after much thought and contemplation, that it was time to retire.

"Our common education is not intended to render us good and wise, but learned."

T. Fuller

Eleven

I was a happy retiree for a month. I thought that I was definitely ready for retirement, but midway through the summer, I realized I was not. For that reason, I accepted a position with the Baltimore County Public Schools and returned to my first love, the classroom. I had learned a great deal during the years when I taught and supervised other teachers, and I was anxious to use the skills I'd learned.

I'd heard that the Baltimore County school system was great, so I was as pleased as punch to teach for the system. It is not wise to believe everything that is rumored. I was interviewed for a teaching position by Dr. P. Brutus, principal of Northeast High School, and Mr. Tyler Marian, the English department chair at the school. They seemed impressed with my experience and credentials. We agreed that I would be assigned a full eleventh-grade teaching schedule. However, I was in for an unpleasant surprise. When school opened, I discovered that I had been assigned three different levels: two eleventh-grade honors classes, one general education tenth-grade class, and two tenth-grade inclusion classes.

Although I'd supervised special education teachers, I'd never taught special education students. The inclusion classes were comprised of special education students and general education students. The academic abilities varied from below average to average. Most of the students had serious behavior problems. Some used their desks as a drum to beat out the rhythm they heard in their heads. Some could barely sit still. Others had anger management issues or oppositional defiant disorder.

Because it was too late to get another assignment, there was nothing I could do about the assignment if I wanted to teach that year. Although I didn't fully understand why my schedule had been changed, I decided to keep the assignment. I discussed the schedule change with the principal, who said the assignment was scheduled by the department chair. So I approached Mr. Marian to discuss the assignment and the instructional materials that I needed.

"Mr. Marian, I am concerned about the change in my schedule."

"Why?" he asked in a condescending tone.

"I prepared all summer for eleventh-grade classes."

"Well, you have what you have. I gave you three honors class."

"You gave me three preparations."

He looked at me with contempt. "Your assignment will not be changed."

Later I found out that the honors classes were not a gift. The students were not honors students. They were just average and below-average struggling students.

I believe that all children can learn. Therefore, I worked hard to teach my assigned classes. I was very concerned about the inclusion classes. I'd observed special ed classes and had taught below-average students many times. I felt that I had sufficient skills, but it certainly would not be easy. Nevertheless, I called a friend who was a special ed teacher and received further information about working with special ed students.

The most challenging problem in teaching these students was the numerous unruly and outlandish behaviors; the school was not strong on discipline. Therefore, although it was difficult, I used rewards and incentives to reach the students and influence their classroom behaviors. My methods worked with some students, but not all. One student in particular, Maddie Hatter, had severe oppositional defiant issues. Her behavior was extremely difficult to manage. I tried all the strategies suggested by the special education department chair and the student's counselor. Nothing seemed to work. Finally, I decided to ignore her behavior. She really didn't like that. One day she came to class and yelled from the back of the room.

"My mother is coming here to see you," she said in threatening tone.

"Why?"

"'Cause I told her about you. She's gonna make you change my grades."

"I don't think so," I said calmly.

"Well, she's gonna talk to the principal."

"And?"

"He's gonna make you."

"I don't think so," I repeated.

"Yes, he is!" she screamed.

I chose to ignore her and continued with the lesson.

"I hate you. I hate you!" she yelled.

I continued to ignore her. She became angrier and started stamping her feet on the floor and singing loudly. I continued to ignore her. She jumped up and down and stomped from her seat to the front of the room, yelling, "I hate you!"

"Miss Hatter, here is your ticket to the office. Hate me there," I said as I handed her a referral to the assistant principal's office. The class laughed. She left, and we continued the lesson.

After months of rewards, incentives, and consistency, I finally gained most of the students' attention. However, it was extremely challenging. I didn't totally win Maddie Hatter's interest, but she improved. I always had a completed referral form prepared. When she announced how much she hated me, I would simply place the referral on her desk, and she would leave, announcing her hatred of me as she passed through the hall en route to the office.

I was very thankful for my experience at the School of Hard Knocks; it prepared me for teaching at Northeast High School. The students were no different there. They didn't hesitate to be rude and disrespectful.

I had assigned a research writing project to my eleventh-grade honors class. One of the students was unhappy with the grade she received and wanted me to know. So she stood and made a loud announcement to the class.

"I worked my ass off for this paper, and she gave me a damn D."

"Oh my dear," I said. "You shouldn't have done that. How will you sit without it?"

The class was in hysterics with laughter. She gave me a harsh stare, rolled her eyes, and mumbled, "She's too damn smart."

Another incident involved a very militant tenth-grade female student named Joesie. She was a tall, thick Caucasian girl who wore camouflage military uniforms, combat boots, and thick, matted dreadlocks. She cursed and threatened me on a regular basis. I tried every strategy that I knew to influence a change in her behavior. Nothing worked. She was mean-spirited and very hostile.

One morning she arrived to class very late and in a foul mood. As she entered the classroom, I glanced in her direction.

"What the f--k you lookin' at me for? So I'm late, so what?"

"Do not speak to me in that tone or use that language."

"I'll talk anyway I want. Make me sick. I can leave, you know."

"Yes, you can and here's your exit ticket out," I said, handing her an office referral.

She stood and stared at me for a moment, snatched the referral out of my hand, walked out, and slammed the door so hard that one of the glass panes in it cracked. The class said, "Damn" in unison.

"Okay, settle down. Let's get back to work," I said.

Finally, I went to see the assistant principal assigned to tenth grade and requested that Joesie be removed from my class.

"Mr. Brown, I have done all that I can do in this matter. Nothing seems to work. When I refer her to your office, you return her to my class without comment."

"I'm not changing her class," he said. "She'll be all right. She just has issues."

"Mr. Brown, I will no longer subject myself to her abuse. If she is not removed from my class, I'll leave. I mean it. She goes, or I go. You decide."

As I turned to leave his office, he said, "Let me see what I can do."

I left his office without looking back. The next morning there was a note in my mailbox from Mr. Brown, informing me that he had moved the student to another class.

I thought about my situation. Again, I was in the new teacher role. Again, I did not receive support from the department chair or the principal. After seeking help a few times and not receiving it, I understood that I was on my own again. I used my skills and was able to complete the year and remain sane. However, at the end of the first semester I informed the principal that I would be leaving at the end of the year and that he should look for a replacement. He was confused. I was very candid, but respectful, as I explained my reasons.

"First, when I was hired I was told that I would teach a complete eleventh-grade schedule. However, when I arrived in September I found that I had been assigned two eleventh-grade honors classes, one tenth-grade regular, and two tenth-grade inclusion classes, which are actually special ed classes. I was assigned an ineffective special education teacher who suffers from the Frank Sinatra syndrome; he wanted to do it his way. Second, the students in the tenth-grade classes have very severe behavior problems, of which you, the department chair, and the other administrators are fully aware."

He looked guilty and started to speak, but I raised my hand in a stop gesture and continued.

"I have been told that these are not special ed students, because they have 504s. By all that is right, all of them should be in special education classes. They not only suffer with ADHD. They also have ABCD, EFGH, IJKL,

MNOP, QRST, UVWX, as well as Y and Z. These students suffer from the entire alphabet.

"Third, I have asked for help with the students' unruly behaviors and have not received it. Finally, when I refer students to the office, they're returned to my class, thumbing their noses at me. I'll stay until the end of the year, but I will not return next year."

Dr. Brutus sat, red-faced, and only said that he was sorry I felt that way. He was not sorry at all, and I knew it. I also knew that my decision to leave Northeast High was best. It was truly a difficult year, but I learned from the experience. I looked forward to leaving the school. Actually, my contract should have expired at the end of the year. However, the human resources specialist had accidentally given me the wrong contract when I was hired, so I had to officially resign. I gladly forwarded the correct forms to the human resource office, and at the end of the year, I happily resigned my position with Baltimore County Public Schools.

Lesson Learned

Not every school principal has principle.

Having resigned from Northeast High School, I now needed a new position. I decided to try substitute teaching. What was I thinking? I refer to my substitute teaching experience as the twilight zone. The very prefix of the word, *sub*, sheds some light on the attitudes of administrators, teachers, parents, and students about the position.

Substitute teachers are considered "less than." They are simply not as respected as other teachers. There seems to be little regard for them. They are paid very little money and given very little support. Most students treat substitutes with little regard, as does the school administration. I tried subbing a couple of times, realized that it was not my forte, and very quickly abandoned the idea.

My next assignment was during the second semester of the same year. I was hired as a temporary administrator in the primary building at Brookfield Elementary School. The students in the primary building were pre-K to grade two. I was looking for a new challenge; I found more than one there. The principal, Mrs. Linda Peoples, asked me to fill in for one of her administrators who was out on sick leave. I'd spoken with Mrs. Peoples in the past about her school, and she'd shared some of the severe behavior problems of students in her primary building. I thought she was probably exaggerating. I thought, *Kids of that age could not behave in such outrageous manners*. I was wrong. They were every bit as disruptive as she had described.

One day a male student was angry because I called his home about his behavior. While he was sitting in the hall waiting for his parent, he decided it would be fun to threaten me.

"Miss Arrrrson, I'ma shoot you in the head."

I ignored him.

"Miss Arrrrson!" he shouted louder, "I'ma shoot you in the eye."

I continued to ignore his threats.

He was really bothered that I continued to ignore him. So he shouted even louder and up an octave.

"Miss Arrrrson, I'ma shoot you in the stomach!"

I stepped into the hall, bent down so as to be almost nose to nose with him, and looked him in the eye. "And you know what I'm going to do, Teddy? I am going to whip your behind."

He sucked in an audible breath, looked shocked, and didn't say another word. He sat quietly until his father came to get him. I told his father about the threats Teddy had made.

Many of the students had severe learning disabilities, and others had terrible behaviors that were difficult to manage. Several took medication for ADHD and other disorders. The situation caused the teachers a great deal of stress because they could not handle the students' behaviors. Therefore, the teachers sent for me fifty times a day to handle the outlandish behaviors that they could not manage. I left work many days with a prize headache. I must say that the principal was very good. She provided many resources for the teachers and she provided training each month. Mrs. Peoples did everything she could to help the students and teachers at her school. It was just a very difficult situation. However, working at Brookfield Elementary was a good experience for me, one I'll always remember. I bonded with most of the teachers and many of the students. I remained at Brookfield Elementary until the end of the school year. The teachers were sorry to see me leave because I was support for them.

At the end of the year I thought, *I am really going to retire this time.* However, I was given the opportunity to teach in an independent Catholic high school. It was too good to pass up. I don't know about other Catholic schools, but this one, Hope High, was a great place to work.

It was an all-girl school. The principal, Sister Rebecca, was one of kindest people I've ever met. She was very professional, with a wonderful soft side. She ran a tight ship but was flexible. She was aware of teachers' needs and provided training for all teachers new to the school.

Not everything was perfect, but there were ample resources available, and order was established. The teachers referred to each other by their first names. Most were very friendly and helpful. The majority of the girls were very well-mannered and respectful.

The first year was great, so when I was invited to return the following year, I gladly accepted. However, during the second year the department chair left to take a position closer to her home, and Mrs. Delores Ditz, a classroom teacher, was assigned as department chair. She had no previous supervisory experience and was very insecure, especially when it came to working with me. I think it may have been because she felt threatened; she knew that I was a retired department head. She did not like anything that I did and constantly attempted to force me to teach using her teaching style. I referred to her privately as Miss Ditzy Doodle. She was very critical of most things I did and often tried unsuccessfully to intimidate me. The fact that I could not be bullied did not make her happy. In addition, she had serious control issues. I found it very difficult to work under her leadership. When at the end of the year I discovered that the school could not offer me a workable schedule for the next year, I saw it as opportunity to leave with grace and dignity, without burning bridges behind me.

I loved being retired because I could pick and choose the positions I wanted. Therefore, I decided to try Baltimore City Public Schools again. I attended a teacher recruitment meeting and met one of my colleagues from Broadside Middle, Mrs. Danielle Starlin. She was the middle school liaison at Broadside and was now principal at the School of Hard Knocks, which had been converted to a middle school. Mrs. Starlin offered me a position as language arts instructional support teacher (IST) at her school. I told her that I did not want to teach on the middle school level. She said that I would not have to teach, so I accepted the offer.

The beginning of the school year was ominous and should have been an indication of what was to come. However, I was excited to return to the school of my first teaching assignment, and I ignored the omen.

When I arrived the first day, I found that I had an office, but it was very dirty and full of junk that needed to be hauled away. I again found myself in a situation in which I would have to clean my work area. Again, I had to wear protective clothes because the place was so nasty. I also had to tag all the junk that needed to be removed. It took two months to clear the space. In the meantime, there were more than ninety-five boxes of books that I was assigned to unpack, stamp, catalog, deliver to teachers, and shelve. Although I reminded Mrs. Starlin of my age, which was sixty-seven, she refused to assign anyone to help me. I was directed to do all the work. I could have refused, but that would have cost me the job, and it was too late to find another. I chose to stay, hoping that it would get better.

I was beginning to notice Dr. Bellicose's character traits in Mrs. Starlin. She exhibited his hateful personality and authoritarian leadership style. She was cold, controlling, malicious, spiteful, and dishonest. Needless to say, I was very disappointed. I'd accepted the position at her request. I thought she was a fair person. However, when I remembered that Dr. Bellicose had trained her, I understood.

Mrs. Starlin was a weak principal. The students were out of control. They walked the halls cursing and yelling. They literally ran up and down the halls. Students called teachers profane names, walked out of class, and did whatever they wanted to do. Not only did they curse the teachers, they cursed Mrs. Starlin too. Furthermore, when teachers referred students to the office, appropriate action was seldom taken. Many teachers were very frustrated and wanted to quit but couldn't afford to do so. Once a male teacher was very angry at a disruptive male student. He almost lost control and hit him. The School of Hard Knocks had been rough when I first taught there, but now it was completely out of control.

One day during the second semester, I was asked to monitor a make-up testing session. I did not know the students and they did not know me. They were accustomed to cursing teachers, so they felt comfortable cursing me. I was called a b--ch so many time that I thought my name had been changed to B--ch Artson. I spoke with the principal about the matter.

"Mrs. Starlin, I have been called b--ch by students this morning more times than I can count."

"Join the club," she said. "I've been called worse."

"I am not joining the club and I'm not going to be called bi-ch anymore. I want something done about the situation. Students should not be allowed to curse teachers. Maybe you don't care if they curse you, but they are not allowed to curse me."

"What do you want me to do? These are kids they send us."

Realizing that she was not going to do anything to change the situation, I was annoyed and left the room.

A couple of weeks later, Mrs. Starlin approached me about taking a full seventh-grade teaching schedule.

"I need you to take the schedule. Failure to do so will probably cause you to lose your job," she said in a patronizing tone.

"Mrs. Starlin, you hired me as an instructional support teacher. You told me at that time that all the new books had been stamped. They had not been stamped. You didn't assign anyone to help me handle the book situation. You did not ask me to be testing coordinator; you had the secretary put a note in my box informing me that testing coordinator is now my duty. You provided no one to assist me with that either. I'm the only testing coordinator in the entire school system who does not have assistance from a committee. I asked for help with the heavy boxes of testing materials. You did not assign anyone to help me with that either. Now you're telling me that you want me to teach a full seventh-grade schedule after telling me when I was hired that I would not have to teach. I am not going to accept the assignment. If I lose my job because I refuse, so be it. Enough is enough. I'd rather keep my health and my sanity."

She listened and allowed me to finish, but her mind was made up. I stared at her for some time. She definitely had Dr. Bellicose's mannerisms. I felt angry and betrayed. I knew that she was taking advantage of me and was trying to bully me as she did some of the other teachers. I decided to quit.

I spoke with someone at the teachers' union, who suggested that I take a leave of absence instead. I applied for the leave and continued the laborious tasks she assigned while waiting for approval. I was scheduled to begin the teaching assignment two weeks after the spring break.

However, I was injured while lifting a heavy box of testing materials and was placed on medical leave. The following year while on leave, I fully and absolutely retired. It was a good decision. Although I miss working with students and teachers, I am now happily retired.

As I look back on all my years as an educator, I smile at the endearing experiences, and I contemplate the mistakes I made. I reminisce with great pleasure as I recall the hundreds of students' lives I had the opportunity to touch. I remember the fascinating people I met and the lasting friendships established.

To those readers considering entering the teaching profession, think carefully about the reasons for your interest. Also, think about the strengths and weaknesses in your character. We all have both. Be as sure as possible that you are willing to make the personal sacrifices required to be successful in the classroom.

To those who are currently in the profession, you have come far. You probably have what it takes. So consider remaining. Consider what you must do to be happy and successful as you continue.

Teaching can be very rewarding. It is not an easy job. However, the impact that teachers make on the lives of young people is lasting. I often encounter adults who I taught as teens and have had the opportunity to realize that I mattered, in and out of the classroom.

Ultimate Lesson Learned

To last in the teaching profession one must have the heart of a lion, the wisdom of Socrates, the physical stamina of Hercules, and the patience of Job.

Teaching is not for wimps.

*" The art of educating requires skill
in fostering a love of mental activity
and a desire of knowledge. "*

E. Kant

Afterthought

New teachers today are still being thrown into nearly impossible situations. They complain about unreasonable expectations, the lack of clear directions, oversize classes, and the scarcity of resources. Moreover, teachers are attacked by unruly and aggressive students each year.

Every year thousands of new teachers leave the profession feeling disappointed and defeated. Many teachers last more than five years, but do not remain in the profession until retirement. They leave for some of the same reasons as new teachers.

The adage, "Those who can, do, and those who can't, teach," is far from true or realistic. There are many good teachers. They work hard and volunteer their time to support their schools. They are creative and inventive risk takers. Without good teachers, there would not be successful people in other professions.

School systems should encourage and support new teachers to prevent them from exiting through the revolving door through which thousands of new teachers depart each year.

I recently discovered that one of the local universities is providing supervising teachers who act as mentors and coaches for selected new teachers. This type of support should be available to all new teachers.

New teachers can acquire strength of will and character, skill, and knowledge by fervently challenging the many obstacles they encounter.

S. Artson

10003302R0

Made in the USA
Lexington, KY
16 June 2011